Audrey and Bill

A Romantic Biography of
AUDREY HEPBURN & WILLIAM HOLDEN

Edward Z. Epstein

RUNNING PRESS
PHILADELPHIA · LONDON

To my incredible sister and brother, Vivian and Steve,
and to our late parents, Rose and Leonard

Books published by Running Press are available at special discounts for
bulk purchases in the United States by corporations, institutions, and other
organizations. For more information, please contact the Special Markets
Department at the Perseus Books Group, 2300 Chestnut Street, Suite 200,
Philadelphia, PA 19103, or call (800) 810-4145, ext. 5000, or e-mail special.
markets@perseusbooks.com.

ISBN 978-0-7624-5597-3
Library of Congress Control Number: 2015930085

E-book ISBN 978-0-7624-5609-3

9   8   7   6   5   4   3   2   1
Digit on the right indicates the number of this printing

Edited by Cindy De La Hoz
Designed by Ashley Haag
Typography: Brand Pro, Neutra Text, and Adobe Caslon

Running Press Book Publishers
2300 Chestnut Street
Philadelphia, PA 19103–4371

Visit us on the web!
www.runningpress.com

CONTENTS

PART III

Chasing Rainbows

PART IV

Here's to Life

PROLOGUE

A YOUNG WOMAN FELL IN LOVE WITH A MARRIED MAN AT their workplace.

Because of her youth, she was romantic and thought she knew more than she did. She had to be romantic, because she'd already had too much reality in her life. Her entire adolescence had been one of deprivation and danger. During those years, her dream was to become a ballerina. She didn't just dream, though. She worked hard at it. But in spite of her discipline and diligence, her much-respected teacher told her that she simply did not have the gift necessary to become a great dancer.

In appearance, she exuded an air of extreme fragility. Her slim frame, huge, almond-shaped hazel eyes, her infectious laugh and genial disposition, her lilting, soft voice, and her impeccable manners gave the impression that, more than anything else in the world, she wanted to please. Yet behind all this was a steely resolve that surfaced in the face of any disappointment.

The workplace that had brought the lovers together was hardly "fun"; in fact, it could be described as hostile, with a tough boss and one particularly irascible, unfriendly, and unsympathetic coworker. Working with such intense individuals proved exhausting, and she was beset by uncertainty, anxiety, and fear. Compounding the situation was the fact that she'd had no formal training for the job she was hired to do. She needed a protector, and there he was; he was a godsend, in a way.

The young woman was Audrey Hepburn, the man was William Holden. And events were on the fast track for both of them.

Audrey's twice-divorced mother, the formidable Baroness Ella van Heemstra Hepburn-Ruston, was upset that her daughter was in a serious relationship with anyone, least of all American film star Holden. He wanted to marry her? For God's sake, he was a married man with three children, although Bill was not the first married man Audrey had been involved with (nor was she the first young actress who had captured his heart).

Powerhouse gossip columnist Hedda Hopper, a woman who could wreck careers, was onto the scent; nothing pleased Hedda more than puncturing the romantic illusions of Hollywood's chosen. Anybody who was "sleeping around" aroused her wrath and her ire, and if Hedda was instrumental in destroying them in the process, "the sons-of-bitches asked for it." Powerful forces at Paramount, and her agents, were protecting Audrey—and Bill—but could only keep the lid on so long. "America's New Sweetheart" (who was not American at all, but European) was tempting fate.

Hepburn and Holden—along with Humphrey Bogart, who disliked them both and didn't hesitate to voice his complaints—were deep into production on the troubled Billy Wilder film *Sabrina*, which had brought the lovers together in the first place. Things were not proceeding smoothly. "Warm up the ice cubes!" Holden would exclaim at the end of a shooting day on most of his films. But, on occasion, there were liquid lunches. Dry martinis were his favorite. As far as director Joshua Logan's experience with Bill was concerned, "He never drank before the end of the shooting day. But once we had reached that part of the day, the gin industry began to prosper. Yet somehow it never seemed to affect him. It did not alter his speech, his wit, or his warmth. He was simply a red-blooded American boy who wanted to have a good time, and believe me, he did."

Audrey liked a good time, too; she had not been in Hollywood very long (*Sabrina* was only her second starring role), and she did not like the place very much. But Holden's outgoing manner and charm were infectious, and she was not accustomed to red-blooded American men. She wasn't an innocent, in fact she was flirtatious and adventurous, and could tell a ribald joke (in a most ladylike fashion, of course).

Bill radiated vitality and virility. He was a gentleman, but there was an edge to him: "I don't know why," he once said, "but danger has always been an important thing in my life—to see how far I could lean without falling, how fast I could go without cracking up."

Holden, his dark hair bleached blond for the film, was just under six feet tall, with a dazzling smile—"His smile could charm the birds out of the trees," noted actress Martha Hyer—and eyes "that were like cornflower-blue sapphires with lights behind them!" Those eyes were constantly focused on Audrey. The sound of his voice was comforting, and his touch seductive. Making movies, especially romantic ones, was about attractive actors gazing at each other, touching each other, day after day, week after week, making intimate relationships almost inevitable. "My God, Audrey and Bill were the most beautiful-to-look-at couple you ever saw!" remarked designer Edith Head. But the Holden situation was poison for Audrey's image—and Bill's. In spite of recent hard-edged roles, he was the idealized All-American Man, in every way: handsome, forthright, sincere, honest, patriotic. And the Ideal Husband, Lover, and Father. But he was wild about Audrey; he had never been happier and didn't seem to care that he was breaking the rules. As he once said, "For me, acting is not an all-consuming thing, except for the moment when I'm actually doing it. There is a point beyond acting, a point where living becomes important."

Audrey's mother, a great beauty in her own right, had spent a lifetime bringing her daughter to this fairy-tale point as a Hollywood princess. During her childhood, Audrey had had to contend not only with the Nazi horror but with a father, a banker, who was a Nazi sympathizer (a fact Audrey's publicity people had so far successfully obscured). But the baroness, with infectious vigor, saw to it that her children's spirits (Audrey had two half-brothers, Alexander and Jan) remained unbroken.

Audrey had recently ended the most serious relationship of her young life, with a dashing British millionaire who wanted to marry her. For many young women, it would have been an easy choice to opt for comfort and security. Audrey chose to pursue her career. "I always wanted to make something of myself," she later declared emphatically.

The road to *Sabrina*—and Bill—hadn't been easy, despite what people thought. Audrey had been a chorus girl, model, film extra, and bit player. One day the French author Colette (*Gigi*) saw her in a hotel, in the south of France working on a British film, and cried out: "There's my 'Gigi'!" The girl was not only smilingly pretty and fresh; she had a velvety voice that was pure as a child's. For Colette, Audrey was a revelation, enchanting, a delicious pleasure. Virtually overnight, she became a star on Broadway in Colette's play, based on the novel.

In contrast, Bill's path to true stardom, which one wag compared to "a salmon swimming upstream," had taken over a decade. His breakthrough to major leading-man status had been relatively recent. When director Billy Wilder cast him, only four years earlier, as the leading man in *Sunset Boulevard*, the industry—and the movie-going public—rediscovered him. In the new era of Marlon Brando and Montgomery Clift, Holden emerged as no longer the boy next door, but a tough contemporary screen presence "guilty of not being innocent." He proved he had the ability to play a cynical, disillusioned character, while remaining vulnerable and likable. In a changing cinema landscape, Holden now fit right in.

In 1954, Audrey and Bill were both in contention for Academy Awards: Audrey, first time out in a major role, as Best Actress for *Roman Holiday*, Bill as Best Actor for *Stalag 17*. It was a well-kept secret that for a key scene in her film, calling for Audrey to cry, it had been necessary to blow menthol into her eyes to produce the required tears. So far, grosses of the film in America were below expectations, but overseas it was a blockbuster. Bill's film was a hit everywhere.

Twenty-four-year-old Audrey had become an instantaneous trendsetter in the fashion world. Her short haircut and doe-eyed makeup were the new rage among women of all ages. Ironically, she not only had serious misgivings about her looks, but, to the consternation of her studio, she voiced them: she thought her nose was too big and did not like her smile. Almost five feet seven without heels, rail-thin at 110 pounds, she had a twenty-inch waist and had redefined the requirement that screen goddesses be petite, curvy, and voluptuous (Marilyn Monroe was at her peak). Director Billy Wilder was quoted: "She might single-handedly make bazooms a thing of the past."

Thanks to Audrey, a boyish silhouette was "in." Even her low-heeled shoes, in an era of high heels, started a trend. She wore them "because I wanted to feel smaller." And there was another reason: the years of ballet had wreaked havoc on her feet—high heels were too painful. She projected a strong sense of self on-screen—she was likable and warm, and exuded an image of manners and attitudes that reflected inner taste and what was then referred to as "breeding."

Now Bill Holden was going to spoil all this? Audrey was the new icon of screen romance. The "romance" designation was fine with her, but the halo of ladylike goodness the press pinned on her both confused and amused her. The designation of home wrecker, however, would be no laughing matter and could potentially annihilate the Cinderella story of the decade. The disapproval of those around her failed to deter Audrey; she was determined and eager to marry Bill Holden, who was wild about her. No matter that he had serious issues of his own; his feelings for Audrey were what they were, and he could hardly be pushed around by the studio. Paramount had a fortune invested in both actors. Holden and Hepburn could very well turn out to be Oscar's Best Actor and Actress of 1953, and teaming them in *Sabrina* was a potential gold mine.

It was the Eisenhower era—Doris Day's bouncy rendition of "I Can't Give You Anything but Love, Baby" was topping the *Billboard* charts— and the illusion of propriety was essential in maintaining the careers of Hollywood gods and goddesses. In addition to Hedda Hopper, and her archrivals Louella Parsons and Sheilah Graham, a new predator was sniffing around: the dreaded *Confidential* magazine, a wildly successful tabloid that paid big bucks to learn "the secret lives of the stars," and damn the consequences. Certain stars' steamy private lives actually helped the box office grosses of their films. "Neither Audrey Hepburn nor Bill Holden were in that group," recalled powerful MCA honcho Jennings Lang. "The public had placed both of them on pedestals, and that was a precarious place to be."

But neither Audrey nor Bill had made it this far by playing it safe.

PART I

Life Will Never Be the Same

Chapter

1

F ROM THE MOMENT AUDREY ARRIVED IN HOLLYWOOD TO prepare for *Sabrina*, before she had even met Bill, one thing was certain—she knew her life was never going to be the same. Expectations were sky-high, and she felt the pressure, personally and professionally. "Don't fuss, dear, just get on with it," was what her mother always told her. But still—in this film, she'd be "on" from Scene 1, when Sabrina's voice begins the picture: "Once upon a time, on the North Shore of Long Island, some thirty miles from New York, there lived a small girl on a large estate. . . ."

There was no shortage of large estates in Beverly Hills, but Audrey was living modestly in what screenwriter Ernest Lehman described as "a nondescript apartment in Westwood." It was a neighborhood bordered by three posh enclaves: Brentwood, Bel Air, and Beverly Hills. Los Angeles gave Audrey culture shock. She was accustomed to cosmopolitan European cities and their way of life. But Hollywood was a small, provincial town devoted to a single obsession—movies, and the people who made them; in addition, it was a goldfish bowl as far as its inhabitants' private lives were concerned. Having the biggest house, the most dazzling jewels, earning the highest salary—these were the governing tenets. Becoming a California resident was never Audrey's plan.

Tinseltown's power hostesses zoned in on Audrey like heat-seeking missiles. Her social pedigree set her apart—in a town full of phonies,

Audrey Hepburn was the real thing, a genuine aristocrat by birth, entitled to call herself a baroness, which she never did, then or later. In an unheard-of gesture to a newcomer, the formidable Doris and Jules Stein (he was founder of MCA) hosted a "Welcome to Hollywood" gala in Audrey's honor at their breathtaking, treasure-filled home. "You had to be a star simply to be a waiter at that party," recalled Jennings Lang. "If you weren't on the guest list, you had to crawl out of town." Mr. and Mrs. Bill Holden, of course, had been on the list, but the couple was away at the time. Hepburn had been forewarned about many things, including Holden—too good-looking, he loves and leaves his leading ladies, then goes back home to his wife.

Audrey would not permit herself to fall into that trap. There would hardly be a shortage of men eager to catch Audrey's eye. She enjoyed socializing and was a seasoned pro at protocol. As she was no stranger to the homes of European aristocrats, the grandeur of Beverly Hills royalty seemed to pale a bit by comparison. Nouveau riche didn't exactly exude the same aura. She became a prized guest at the sprawling ten-acre estate of Jack and Ann Warner. If one hoped to win an Oscar, socializing was essential, and Audrey wanted to win. She was a refreshing new face and, amazingly, was neither affected nor arrogant. She actually seemed grateful for the interest in her. She had a sense of humor, too—when a waiter edged a tray past nearby Peter Lawford's head, she playfully cautioned: "Look out for your head, Mr. Lawford!"

"Is she for real?" wondered observers. "Isn't she a duchess or something?" Her *Roman Holiday* co-star, Gregory Peck, described her not as regal, but "spunky . . . a very lovable girl who would make faces and clown."

The utter simplicity of her look was in stark contrast to the ultra-bejeweled, sequined, elaborately coiffed female denizens occupying the highest levels of Hollywood society. She shook a lot of hands, smiled brightly, and spoke quietly and modestly. Everyone seemed to know each other, exchanging anecdotes and laughing heartily at them; sometimes Audrey was completely bewildered, with no idea what they were talking about, but she laughed, too. Everyone seemed to want to overwhelm her with their charm.

Columnist Doris Lilly, thirty-one-year-old California-born author of the best-seller *How to Marry a Millionaire*, was a tall, sexy blonde who took note of new arrivals on the New York and Hollywood scenes. (Ms. Lilly was the inspiration for Truman Capote's Holly Golightly character in *Breakfast at Tiffany's*.) "It's always the sweet, innocent-looking, ethereal types, the Audrey Hepburns, who are the real potential threats to Hollywood wives," noted Lilly.

The start date for *Sabrina* was approaching, and Audrey concentrated on all the things she must do; she felt conscious of herself as "Audrey Hepburn," an illusion in the public eye, created out of her own work, publicity photographs, ever-present currents of gossip, the whole Cinderella myth. There had been *A Star Is Born*–type layouts in *Life* and *Look* magazines. There had been speculation, before *Sabrina* was set, that she'd be Brando's leading lady in *Désirée*; Joseph L. Mankiewicz wanted her to star in his proposed film of Shakespeare's *Twelfth Night*.

But Audrey was unusual in that she didn't fall into the trap of believing her own publicity, which had ensnared many actors. Her broad perspective was no doubt a legacy of her horrendous World War II experiences. She wouldn't discuss those years but suffered from anemia as a result of them and had seen one of her half-brothers sent to a labor camp. None of it was something she felt should be linked to publicity.

She could appreciate the irony that while she'd spent years studying ballet and never became a dancer, she hadn't spent any time studying acting and was becoming a movie and stage star.

The intrusiveness of the press made her uncomfortable. Reporters had insinuated, incorrectly, that she had been the cause of the breakup of *Roman Holiday* co-star Gregory Peck's marriage. From then on, her byword regarding the media was caution. Her attitude gave her an aura of reserve, which had the effect of making the press even more curious: what was she *really* like?

∼•∽

Bill could not wait to meet Audrey. She'd captivated him in *Roman Holiday*. He saw a radiance in her that he knew couldn't have been faked by even the most gifted director and cameraman. He was actually nervous at the prospect of working with her—what if there was no chemistry between them? And what if that quality she had on-screen only came through on-screen? Experience had taught him that that was not uncommon. He would trust his instincts—he was older and felt that he was wiser than she.

As Audrey would discover, Bill's background—like hers—was intriguing, not standard Hollywood stuff. He was not a street kid who'd had to claw his way to respectability. His reasonably well-to-do family's roots traced back to George Washington's mother, and he was always proud of the fact that he was distantly related to "one of the founders of our country." Bill was Irish-English-German, "mixed in an American shaker," as he liked to say. His maternal grandfather was a cousin of Warren G. Harding, twenty-ninth president of the United States.

Bill had been born William Franklin Beedle Jr. in O'Fallon, Illinois, on April 17, 1918. When he was three, the family moved to Pasadena, California. His father, William, was an industrial chemist; his mother,

Mary, a teacher. He had two younger brothers, Robert (Bob) Westfield Beedle, and Richard (Dick Porter) Beedle.

It would come as no surprise to Audrey to learn that Bill had been a rebellious kid, a restless spirit. He was driven to prove himself to his father, who never told Bill that he loved him (Audrey was convinced that her own father had never loved her). Beedle Sr. was a tall, good-looking man with a knockout smile, a former amateur gymnast who'd taught his sons how to tumble, box, and keep physically fit.

Young Bill had been fearless—wire walking on telephone lines; racing his motorcycle—he once even did a handstand on top of the Aurora Bridge in Pasadena. There was nothing of that nature he wouldn't try, either in his youth or as an adult. Terrified onlookers, including current pals from the movie business, didn't realize that he actually knew what he was doing, and his expertise would come in handy for a crucial confrontation scene between him and Bogart in *Sabrina*.

Moss Hart once described the theater as "the inevitable refuge for the unhappy child." In 1937, a Paramount talent scout had spotted nineteen-year-old Bill portraying an eighty-year-old in a Pasadena Playhouse production; the studio signed him to a contract. Even after that, his father still wanted him to become a chemist, like him. Beedle Sr. never forgave his son, and in years to come, when Bill was in his thirties, he would sadly describe his parents' relationship with him as "detached."

While young Bill was learning the ropes at Paramount, his brother Bob enlisted as a pilot in the naval air corps. Inspired by his younger brother, Bill too wanted to join the service; Paramount wouldn't release him from his contract. But after the 1941 bombing of Pearl Harbor, Bill was the first married star to enlist. One night, sound asleep in the barracks, Bill awoke from a nightmare, overwhelmed by a feeling that something horrible had happened. The feeling lingered for days, and on January 4, 1944, he learned that his brother's plane had been shot down. Bob was dead. It was a heart-wrenching time for Bill, his surviving brother, and their parents. Bill, as always, kept his sorrow to himself.

To the world at large, Bill seemed forthright and uncomplicated, but his striking good looks and personal charm were deceiving. They masked a very complex nature, although actor Cliff Robertson, a close friend in later years, had another opinion: "Bill didn't seem that complex to me. I think he simply felt out-of-sync with a complicated environment."

Audrey was accustomed to complicated environments, and she seemed to be coping well enough with the current one. Even before they met, Bill empathized with her predicament—sudden stardom, and the pressures it brought, which were not at all what people thought. He was curious to find out how Audrey was handling it all with such aplomb. Or was she? The young Bill in 1937, like the young Audrey who had just arrived in Hollywood, had virtually no acting experience. As Paul Newman once said about the actor's art, "It's like being stark naked, in front of an audience, and having to turn around very, very slowly. . . ."

Bill had experienced that feeling firsthand, at twenty-one, when, after making a couple of minor movies, he landed the title role in the film version of Clifford Odets's highly lauded play, *Golden Boy*, in which he would portray a young man torn between becoming a violinist or a boxer. If it hadn't been for the intervention of the film's star, Barbara Stanwyck, he would have been fired, but instead he succeeded and for years *Golden Boy*, released in 1939, typed Holden as the screen's "All-American Boy." Stanwyck was fourteen years older than Bill, had been a star for almost a dozen years, and became, in effect, Bill's protector and confidante. He was forever grateful; every year thereafter he sent her dozens of roses on her birthday.

Almost forty years after *Golden Boy*, at the 1978 broadcast of the Oscars, Holden appeared onstage with Stanwyck and emotionally paid tribute to her, describing her as "a lovely human being" and explaining how "her interest, and understanding, and professional integrity, and her encouragement, and above all her generosity" had enabled him to succeed. She was overcome. "Oh, Bill," she said, hugging him.

After being discharged from the service, the Golden Boy faced tough times professionally. He was no longer a "boy," and he had a family to support. Son Peter was born in 1943, and Scott in 1946. His wife, Ardis, had been an actress under contract to Warner Bros. The studio tried making her a star and renamed her Brenda Marshall, but she gave up her career to become a full-time wife and mother. Of these years, when Bill couldn't afford to buy his growing family a larger house, Holden said, "If I hadn't had a family, I would not have found the strength to go on." But cracks had begun appearing in their marriage, and Ardis told friends that giving up her career might not have been such a great idea.

It was not until 1950, five years after being discharged from the service, that Bill played Joe Gillis in *Sunset Boulevard* and thus reached A-list stardom. Bill was nominated for an Oscar for his performance but lost to José Ferrer in *Cyrano de Bergerac*. *Stalag 17*, Holden's next film directed by Wilder, would change all that.

The year 1954 was extraordinarily good for Bill. Fifteen years after *Golden Boy*, Holden starred with none other than his darling "Missy" Stanwyck and his childhood idol, Fredric March, in MGM's all-star production of *Executive Suite*. Working with Stanwyck again brought him the kind of satisfaction that was usually lacking in his professional life. He was deeply moved to see her so proud of him. "I told you!" she said.

As for Fredric March—he was pleasant enough, and, surprisingly, had a playful sense of humor. He got a kick out of the fact that Holden had been a young fan of his, and in later years would offer Bill valuable career advice. A longtime Holden girlfriend, blonde bombshell Shelley Winters, also had a starring role in the film. Even though Bill's good looks were hard to ignore, "By this time, our relationship was history," recalled Winters.

The extent of Audrey's success, after only one screen vehicle, was reflected in the fact that for *Sabrina*, she was to receive billing above the experienced Holden. Billing was at the discretion of their studio, Paramount. Holden wasn't thrilled with this—he felt that Paramount, after a dozen years, was still treating him as new kid on the block.

There were actors who actually counted the number of lines they had in a script, judging their importance to the project accordingly. Bill Holden was hardly in this group, yet he was acutely aware that a studio could sabotage any player if and when it wanted to. Warner Bros., for example, was notorious for breaking expensive star contracts by delivering inferior scripts it knew the actor would have to turn down, if he or she hoped to maintain status. Bette Davis and Humphrey Bogart were stellar examples of this practice.

Happy-go-lucky attitude aside, Bill *cared*. He was on a roll, but never for a moment did he doubt that his, or any star's, future, was at best uncertain. "Bill was certain he'd wake up one day and discover the whole thing was one big joke," said his pal, actor Robert Mitchum.

It was no joke to Audrey—star billing and the star treatment were the least of her concerns at this moment. She was still adjusting to having ended her relationship with fiancé James Hanson, a British baron. It had been unpleasant. He was handsome, wealthy (the family owned a trucking firm); he had said he loved her and had made frequent trips to be by her side. He once flew to New York when she was appearing on Broadway in *Gigi*, and the couple was photographed all over town, including enjoying the sights at Rockefeller Center. But, obviously, Hanson did not understand what drove her. He expected Audrey to retire and be content as his wife. If his intention was to make her jealous by being seen and photographed in European nightclubs and at top restaurants with various beauties, he miscalculated. The baroness had urged her daughter to move on, although she would later admit that at least Hanson did not have the complication of a wife and children that Holden had.

On top of everything else, Audrey had to contend with the fact that she was the envy of her peers. It had taken Bill over a dozen years to reach that level; but what exactly had young Audrey done to deserve such sudden, extravagant success? Many of Hollywood's veterans resented her; they felt she had not paid any dues. First, Gregory Peck as a leading man; now, for *Sabrina,* Cary Grant and Bill Holden had been announced as her co-stars. (It should be noted, Audrey's salary, meanwhile, was not remotely in the league of her co-stars, who were earning more than twenty times what she was, but her agents would soon rectify this.) And to have Billy Wilder as her next director! First the celebrated William Wyler, on *Roman Holiday,* now Wilder.

So far she had been incredibly lucky, she knew that—but why didn't people realize she had indeed worked hard to reach this point? She was coming off a workload that would have overwhelmed many of her contemporaries. Marilyn Monroe struggled merely to complete a film shot at her home studio in Hollywood. Hepburn had no sooner finished *Roman Holiday* in Rome, a very difficult four-month shoot, during stiflingly hot and humid weather, when, immediately afterward, she embarked on an arduous cross-country tour of the United States in *Gigi,* a contractual commitment she could not break.

Through it all, she often felt unwell and was grateful that her mother was there to watch over her. The *Gigi* company played major cities from coast to coast, including a two-week run at the Biltmore Theater in Los Angeles. Warm applause from a live audience and signing autographs for admiring fans was hardly unpleasant, but acting was not second nature to her; she was learning her craft while the world watched (as had Holden, who had great respect for the fact that Audrey was successful on the stage).

She took the profession of acting, whether onstage or in front of a camera, very seriously. Bernard Drew, a writer and critic of film and theater, later made an interesting observation: "Audrey was not a great stage actress—she was a *presence* onstage. In the two roles I saw her do—'Gigi' and, later, 'Ondine,' she was exactly right in type for those parts, to such an extent that it made up for her lack of technique as a stage actress. Claudette Colbert, for example, was an even better stage actress than she was in films. But movies were the ideal medium for Audrey—she was made for them." And she preferred them—though circumstances could be unpredictable.

A week before production on *Sabrina* was to begin, the trade papers announced that Cary Grant might not do the film. Was this how Hollywood worked? Audrey was surprised, disappointed, and worried. Grant was perfect casting for the role of the urbane, serious, workaholic, worldly-wise older brother, Linus Larabee, who ultimately ends up competing with his playboy brother (Holden) for Sabrina's affections. She was thrilled at the prospect of working with both actors. But Grant had had reservations all along: was he too old to be her leading man? He was fifty. Would neophyte Audrey become the object of most of the director's efforts? Furthermore, Wilder and Holden had already worked together successfully on two films and knew each other well— where would that leave Cary? Despite Billy Wilder's impassioned pleas, Grant withdrew.

Enter Humphrey Bogart, whose career had been reborn, big-time, with his Academy Award–winning performance two years earlier in *The African Queen*. He was in demand at all the studios, and he was the last-minute replacement for Grant. Despite murmurings of miscasting, Bogart was a smart choice. The excitement about the trio of stars for *Sabrina* was maintained. But with "Bogie" came other problems—he resented the fact that he was second choice; he was wary of playing romantic comedy, which was Cary Grant's forte, not his (that had been one of the studio's major concerns); and at fifty-four, he was thirty years older than his inexperienced leading lady (and offscreen he more than looked it) and twenty years older than Bill Holden, his "rival" for Sabrina's affections.

"Don't worry about it, I'm rewriting the part for you. You'll be great! Trust me," enthused Wilder. Besides rewriting, the director warned cameraman Charles Lang not to backlight Bogart, who tended to "spit" out his lines, literally. But Bogart had reservations about Wilder: they had never worked together before, and he was accustomed to pals like director John Huston, whose laconic style was the antithesis of Wilder's. And finally, unknown to Wilder and virtually anyone else, other than his wife, Lauren Bacall, Bogart was not in the best of health (he was to die four years later).

Bogart and Bacall had co-starred in hit films, and there were even comments that Bogart felt Bacall should be playing Sabrina. His marriage to Bacall, who was twenty-five years younger, negated any undue attention to the age differential between Bogie and Hepburn. If he could be married in real life to a gorgeous, much younger woman and have two children with her, it made perfect sense that a younger woman would be attracted to him on-screen. Of course, it was unimaginable that a female star Bogart's age would be cast opposite a leading man Audrey's age, with the couple getting married and living happily ever after.

Fortunately for Audrey, there was a mutual admiration society between her and Billy Wilder. They had personal history in common: the Nazis had directly affected both their lives. Born in 1906 in Sucha Beskidzka, Austria-Hungary, Wilder, who was Jewish, had fled to America in 1933 after the rise of the Nazi Party. At the time he was making *Sabrina*, Billy was forty-seven, a head shorter than Audrey, and bursting with vitality and enthusiasm. He was one of Paramount's platinum talents, an Oscar-winning writer-producer-director of extraordinary ability and versatility: his prior successes included several screen classics, including *Double Indemnity, The Lost Weekend,* and his two hits with Holden, *Sunset Boulevard* and *Stalag 17.* Wilder was very much looking forward to working with Bill again—and with Audrey. He even gave Audrey a present that she loved: a bicycle, which had been her major source of transportation back home.

Chapter

2

"HOW'S THE SCRIPT COMING?" ASKED BILL HOLDEN, ANX-
ious, as always, when the time to begin a new film was at hand.
"Great!" Wilder replied. "It's going to be your best part so far!"

"And Audrey—what's she like?"

"You're going to love her. She asked me what you're like!"

Holden, for personal reasons, was not happy about the Bogart casting. Bogart and Holden had worked together years before, not harmo-
niously, in *Invisible Stripes*, which was made the year Holden did *Golden
Boy*. Bogart, a showbiz veteran even back then, proved to be no Barbara
Stanwyck as far as offering help and support to neophyte Holden, who
was top-billed. Perhaps there was more to the animus between them.
Bogart was always tuned in to the gossip that permeated the filmmaking
world and was most likely aware that young Holden had, in Holden's own
words decades later, "serviced" some older actresses to further his career.
In response to probing questions from his psychoanalyst, Holden further
explained: "I'm a whore. All actors are whores. We sell our bodies to the
highest bidder."

Artistic temperaments aside, Wilder reassured him that *Sabrina*
would be a triumph for all concerned. Paramount had paid top dollar
for the screen rights to Samuel Taylor's play, *Sabrina Fair*, before it even
opened. It became a great Broadway success for Margaret Sullavan, who
was forty-four—Audrey's senior by twenty years. Sullavan was magical

onstage, critics loved her, and she would be a hard act to follow. She was aware when she'd signed for the play that she would not have the film role—that would be for either twenty-two-year-old Elizabeth Taylor or twenty-five-year-old Jean Simmons.

Some said Audrey had read the play and asked Paramount to buy it for her. *Roman Holiday* director William Wyler was Sullavan's ex-husband. "Now Willie's discovery gets the role that I have made a success," remarked Sullavan. "C'est la vie!" she joked, but one assumes she wasn't laughing; nor were Joseph Cotten and Scott McKay, both losing the roles they originated to Bogart and Holden.

The film adaptation of *Sabrina* had become a chaos of rewrites. Billy Wilder had been collaborating with playwright Taylor in rewriting his creation to make an appropriate vehicle for the film's stars, trying to craft it to work for audiences in Omaha as well as New York City. Screenwriter Ernest Lehman was hired to further rework the material, especially Audrey's role. A mild nervous breakdown awaited Lehman at the completion of his assignment.

Bill Holden had no problem waiting for a final shooting script. He trusted Wilder; Wilder was a man who understood and knew how to use the contradictions in Bill's nature. Bill's agents, no doubt, would raise holy hell about any delays. They had Bill booked years into the future. But Bill welcomed an occasional respite from the sound stages; the thrill of acting was beginning to wear thin.

Meanwhile, Audrey was in the midst of fighting a crucial preproduction battle. She was extremely conscious of her clothes, and that "simple" look she achieved was the result of careful thought and lavish, time-consuming attention to invisible detail. She had no illusions that she would look beautiful no matter who did her clothes. Quite the opposite; she was self-conscious about her skinny upper body (refusing ever to wear "falsies") and felt she was awkwardly proportioned. It was a source of wonder to her that so many women envied her figure.

Audrey ended up being aided and abetted by Billy Wilder. For plot reasons, Wilder wanted the character of Sabrina, from a certain point on, to wear a genuine Paris couture wardrobe. Audrey was looking forward to her costumes being created by her beloved new friend, twenty-six-year-old rising French couturier Hubert de Givenchy, whose family tree bore similarities to Audrey's, Givenchy being a marquis. Theirs had been a meeting of souls. He was very tall and towered over Hepburn, but he was soft-spoken, charming, and handsome. He totally understood, sympathized, and empathized with Audrey's doubts and fears. "I feel protected in his clothes," she said.

Designer approval was not in her contract. Diminutive Edith Head had created Audrey's Oscar-winning wardrobe for *Roman Holiday*. Although the neophyte had insisted, politely but firmly, on many refinements, Edith had done a masterful job. She was not only the undisputed empress of fashion on the Paramount lot, having been there since the 1920s, but she fiercely maintained and guarded her position. "One did not cross Edith Head without fear of reprisal," noted fashionista-executive Anita Colby. "There were things she could do. . . ."

Audrey used all her considerable diplomatic skills dealing with Edith Head. It was tense and tedious work. On top of it all, Givenchy had told Audrey he could not do her costumes for the film: "There are too many of them. I have only eight seamstresses, and I have other clients."

"You will do them," Audrey said.

"You'd better learn fast to roll with the punches, or you're cooked," Bill Holden once said. "That is, if you expect to have a long career."

Hepburn was learning to do just that—even if she had become the prima ballerina she had always yearned to be, Audrey would have discovered the same jealousies, competitiveness, intrigue, and backstabbing that lurked in the movie world, as it lurks in every profession. This was a pivotal time for her; by the time she'd been nominated for an Oscar and was making her second big studio film, she was not the unknown wonder anymore. She had to prove herself—prove that *Roman Holiday* had not been a flash in the pan. While appearing capable and calm, inside she was deeply insecure, which made her nervous. Waiting for a start date on *Sabrina*, to keep panic at bay, she chain-smoked and gave in to an occasional crying spell, a sure sign of the underlying tension that is often present in artists.

The delays kept Audrey on edge. She liked to reflect on the character she was playing, and the situations the character was involved in; she wasn't able to switch her emotions on and off before and after playing a scene, as, for example, Bette Davis could. Billy Wilder was aware of this and did his best to put her at ease. When he met with her to discuss the evolving script, in which he was tailoring the character of Sabrina to reflect Audrey's personality, Wilder would tell her tales of old Hollywood. His Mitteleuropa delivery made her laugh, and with Audrey, laughing was always the best medicine. It helped to get her through this difficult time.

Audrey would be required to sing a brief song in *Sabrina*—an intimate rendition of the French ballad "La Vie en Rose." No orchestral or even piano accompaniment would be added on the soundtrack. It was a song that, as Audrey's character explains, was the French way of saying "looking at life through rose-colored glasses." The singing scene would take place with her seated alongside Bogart as he drove a convertible. She worked as hard on learning how to sing as she did on studying ballet. Frederick Hollander, who worked with Marlene Dietrich on developing her abilities as a chanteuse, was Audrey's coach. When the time came to pre-record the song, she delivered a flawless rendition, pitch-perfect and seemingly effortless. Her singing voice sounded exactly like her speaking voice, and Billy Wilder was delighted—Audrey had that something extra, even when she sang.

She viewed her hair-and-makeup tests with a highly critical eye, cognizant that hers was not a perfect face—nor was she crazy about the way her teeth looked when she smiled. She knew how vital a film's cameraman was—he was the person who determined how she looked on-screen. It was no accident that some stars, such as Jean Harlow and Merle Oberon, had married their cameramen.

Audrey was very pleased with veteran cinematographer Charles Lang, whom the front office had cautioned to "watch out for Ms. Hepburn's bony shoulders." She'd been so unhappy on seeing photographs of herself during *Roman Holiday* that she chose not to watch daily "rushes" of the film. She was fortunate to be working with Lang; these early films established the basis for her on-screen image, one that would endure for the next several decades and beyond.

Audrey's insecurities about her looks were not totally unfounded. Cecil Beaton, the renowned, at times controversial British photographer/set-and-fashion designer, who was the ultimate word on taste, had privately assessed newcomer Audrey. He thought it "a rare phenomenon to find a young girl with such inherent 'star' quality," her stance a combination "ultra-fashion plate and ballet dancer." He further described her as "a new type of beauty: huge mouth, flat Mongolian features, heavily painted eyes, a coconut coiffure, long nails without varnish, a wonderfully lithe figure, a long neck, but perhaps too scraggy." He noted that her great success in *Roman Holiday* had made "little impression on this delightful human being," and he was impressed that she responded to the adulation "with a pinch of salt: gratitude rather than puffed-up pride. . . . In a flash I discovered [her] sprite-like charm, and she has a sort of waif-ish, poignant sympathy." Beaton and Hepburn would work together a decade later, on *My Fair Lady*.

Although many young stars resented the strictures of the studio system, Audrey was comfortable with it. It was in harmony with her innate discipline. Paramount was both effective and efficient in dealing with many of her concerns; the studio was immensely helpful handling matters regarding her passport, working papers, and so on. At a moment's notice, there was transportation by limousine; tickets—for the theater, airline, and so on—could be obtained that wouldn't be easily available otherwise, with VIP treatment across the board; the publicity department kept unwanted news hounds away (and finessed them when unwanted questions arose) and routinely planted laudatory stories in the press. Studio photo sessions "killed" unflattering images (cigarettes were usually airbrushed out of approved on-set photos). One could count on the studio to recommend and set up appointments with the proper dentist, or doctor, or, if emergencies arose, "take care of things." Jean Howard Feldman, as high on Hollywood's "in" list as one could get, said that, during this period, studios could arrange literally anything: "Certain actors, and others, obtained their drivers' licenses without ever having to take a driver's test." Audrey, along with Monroe, Kim Novak, James Dean, Rock Hudson, Grace Kelly, and a select few others, would be among the last to flourish under this system.

Yet, amid all this attention and activity, Audrey was aware of something missing: a special man.

~•~

Audrey was a woman who needed the man to make the first move. A potential new prince charming, pre–Bill Holden, had appeared in Audrey's life, and though he did move first, he didn't sweep her off her feet. They had met in London prior to her coming to Hollywood for *Sabrina*. Gregory Peck introduced them, and she definitely found him attractive. He was thirty-six, a lean six feet three, and American (born in New Jersey). An ambitious actor-writer-producer-director, everything about him was cosmopolitan, and many people assumed he was European.

Recently he'd starred in one of Audrey's favorite movies (she saw it three times), a charming musical fantasy, *Lili*, about a puppeteer in love with a young woman who is unaware of his deep feelings for her; he expresses his feelings through his puppets. The picture was a hit, running for over a year at an art house in New York, but it had not made him a major star. Leslie Caron, a young French actress not unlike Audrey in gamine appeal, played the girl; Mel Ferrer was the puppeteer.

Although there was mutual attraction between them, it was hardly love at first sight for Audrey. Ferrer was persistent, though, and accompanied her to New York for the opening of *Roman Holiday*. She found his ideas about her career, the kind of roles she should play, challenging and interesting. But there was a complication: Mel was married, with children. Anticipating a possible future with Audrey, he contemplated divorcing his third wife, who had, in fact, been his first wife; they had remarried after he divorced wife number two. (Talk about the complication of having a wife!)

The Cinderella Girl faced an additional dilemma: others before her had to contend with it, often with disastrous results, as would future Cinderellas. When a young actress ascends to breathtaking career heights, she becomes a magnet for all sorts of individuals eager to move in on and capitalize on such success—people who will say or do anything. The wise novice learns to trust no one; if she can cope with that anxiety-producing fact, without plunging into a pit, she is lucky. Audrey's luck, to some extent, was her mother. The baroness wasn't crazy about Mel.

In any case, he was pushed to the back of Audrey's mind—and he certainly was not in her heart—as she steeled herself for her first day's work on *Sabrina*.

Chapter

3

B ILL, BORED WITH WAITING FOR PRODUCTION TO BEGIN, became obsessive over the prospect of meeting Hepburn. He hoped she was a Holden fan, but he was prepared for the possibility that she hadn't even seen any of his pictures. "Before I even met her, I had a crush on her," said William Holden, "and after I met her, just a day later, I felt as if we were old friends, and I was rather fiercely protective of her, though not in a possessive way."

At least he didn't think he was possessive. Audrey liked him at first sight and later said he was the handsomest man she had ever met. The sparks between them were evident to all. Bill was good-humored and thoroughly masculine. He gave off a stimulating aura that was both warm and electric. He could offer her comfort and excitement in the same package. She sensed, and perhaps hoped, that something wonderful was going to happen.

As far as the task at hand: if the old Hollywood adage was true—that a happy set usually resulted in a lousy picture—than *Sabrina* had no worries. There would be misery aplenty. "Nobody sets out to make a bad picture," Bogart had noted in the course of his very long career. "But it's miraculous when a good result emerges." William Holden had his own approach: "Take any picture you can. One out of four will be good, one out of ten will be very good, and one out of fifteen will get you an Oscar."

Sabrina was trouble from day one, and Audrey was grateful Bill was on the scene. The first couple of days on any film are nerve-wracking. The tension is palpable, insecurities come out in the open, tempers flare, and everyone is scared. As George Cukor once noted, "If anything gets on film that first day that is usable, it's a miracle."

Stamina has always been a basic requirement for getting through the long months of a film shoot. The days, and occasionally nights, are filled with starting the flow of emotions, then stopping it, then waiting interminably before having to start it up again. The actors, then as now, have to report to the studio as early as 5:00 a.m., which means getting up around 4:00 a.m. In the time of *Sabrina*, there were "watchdogs" all over—that is, spies, whose job was to observe and report to the front office on how much progress was being made, or not made, and on anyone who might not be behaving in the best interests of the studio. Progress on a film is usually slow and tedious. It is unusual to get a shot by 9:00 a.m. The actors must deal with perspiration, humidity (a nightmare for hairstylists), and makeup streaking under hot lights, all requiring constant repairs. It is an enervating business calling for discipline and patience. Actor David Niven once remarked, "Making movies? It's a world of heightened emotions, a search for satisfaction on all levels. Production must go smoothly, deadlines must be met. Stars must be kept happy, beautiful, and functioning at top capacity." The front office's credo was simple: "Whatever it takes."

"Bill never thought of himself as much of an actor," said his close friend of later years, actor Cliff Robertson. "Hard to believe, considering his body of work, but that's how he felt." Former Holden co-star Nancy Olson later observed that she felt Bill was uncomfortable with the fact that there was "a certain narcissism in making movies. It demands a kind of vanity that is not natural."

Bogart's vanity was taking a clobbering—he was painfully aware of his own physical shortcomings on this shoot. It had not mattered how he looked for his tour-de-force portrayal of the weather-beaten, hard-edged-but-with-a-heart-of-gold captain of the *African Queen;* his leading lady, Katharine Hepburn (no relation to Audrey), was in her forties, and for the film, devoid of all superficial Hollywood glamour. Under John Huston's direction, Bogie—and Katharine—pulled out all stops in delivering two of the most memorable performances in cinema history, despite the considerable physical hardships of filming on location in a real jungle. On *Sabrina,* filmed in the cloistered environment of a top Hollywood studio, it mattered very much how Bogart looked; he knew it, and he was very nervous about it. The makeup and hair departments labored mightily to produce a believable leading man for a leading lady young enough to be his daughter. Some even said she looked like she could be his granddaughter. Cameraman Charles Lang's lighting and camera angles were as carefully contrived as a Swiss watch movement.

Compounding Bogie's dilemma was Bill Holden, whose youthful good looks soon became, over the course of production, the butt of many sarcastic Bogart remarks. When Billy Wilder had said to Gloria Swanson during production of *Sunset Boulevard* that she looked "too young" opposite Holden, she retorted, only half joking: "Make him look older!" Bogart thought Bill was more a matinee idol than an actor, and ridiculed his bleached-blond hair, which was a cosmetic change for this picture ordered to emphasize the contrast between the two brothers. Bogie's buzz cut was a hairpiece; Bill's thick head of hair, bleached or not, was his own. Holden was not immodest; he knew he was great looking and was proud of it.

Embarking on *Sabrina,* neither Holden nor Bogart had forgotten their hostile working experience on *Invisible Stripes.* The two stars did have two things in common: both were competitive and were serious drinkers. And both of them led directly to starting *Sabrina* off on the wrong foot. At the end of the first shooting day, Bogie invited select members of cast and crew for drinks in his dressing room, excluding three major players: Billy Wilder, Audrey, and Bill, whom he had decided were out to sabotage him. The game-playing had begun. Because Wilder and Holden were close pals, and new-kid-on-the-block Audrey was being looked out for by both of them, where did that leave Bogie?

Meanwhile, because Bogart had excluded Audrey, Wilder, and him from drinks in his dressing room, Holden responded by inviting Audrey, Wilder, Ernest Lehman, and others for drinks in his dressing room—an invitation not extended to "Mr. Bogart."

Bogart was well aware that during the first two weeks of a shoot, any actor—including a star—could be replaced. But after that, everyone was locked in. In the ensuing weeks, Audrey saw the set of her new movie turn into a battleground. After making *Roman Holiday,* she had said: "Out of that curious studio life of camera, lights, noises, and nerves, I had to try to bring a true performance." She said it had been the most trying time of her life.

Until now, that is. Audrey, Bill, and Wilder would remain front and center in Bogart's line of fire. Hepburn, Holden, and Wilder would be referred to by Bogart, before the shoot was over, as "you Paramount bastards." Audrey diplomatically kept her emotional distance from the turmoil as much as possible. But it was not easy. The explosion of temperaments was harrowing. For her, this was no *Roman Holiday.* But *Roman Holiday* hadn't introduced her to Bill.

Many a weak director fell victim to the actors. "A director—a serious director, not a director of television or something like that—it eats you inside," Wilder said many years later, bluntly explaining: "You just have to absorb so much. And the thing is that you have to swallow so much shit from people. It's a very, very simple formula. You've got to live with them, once you've started with them. Because if the picture is half finished, if there's anything wrong, they're gonna throw me out, not one of the actors."

Bogart's agent said that Bogie didn't realize that the real star of a Billy Wilder film was Billy Wilder. For this director, it was vital that there be no question about who was boss. Boundaries had to be established. Wilder was a tough, clever, acerbic man. He'd survived in the Hollywood jungle as long as Bogart. Billy was furious at the studio, which had balked at his terms for a new contract. This was going to be his last film for Paramount, after eighteen years of service, and he was determined to show up those front-office bastards by leaving with a smash hit as his swan song. In the process he would have to swallow— up to a point—whatever Bogie shoveled his way; but at least he had the unwavering support and confidence of Audrey and Bill. And, in Bogart, he knew he actually had one of the screen's great lovers—Bogie had, after all, played Rick in *Casablanca*.

As far as Audrey was concerned, her survival instinct clicked into gear. It was ironic, considering that Bogart was hardly a stranger to properly showcasing a new actress. He and director Howard Hawks had lavished unlimited patience, and extreme care, in presenting Bronx-born Betty Persky (renamed Lauren Bacall) in her first film, *To Have and Have Not,* which starred Bogart. Bacall said the experience spoiled her for future movies because she thought every movie would be run that way. There was a crucial difference, of course, between Betty and Audrey—Bogart fell madly in love with Betty. He did not recognize or outwardly acknowledge the fact that Bacall and Audrey shared common ground: both were young, slim, and tall for actresses (Bacall at five feet eight, Hepburn at five feet seven), with mannequin-like figures.

And both were obsessed with high fashion. It leads one to wonder how *Sabrina* would have turned out if Bogart had fallen under Audrey's spell the way most people did.

Holden, of course, had a perfect relationship with Wilder, who had rescued him from post–World War II cinema oblivion by casting him in *Sunset Boulevard*—which made Holden an Oscar nominee—and having recently directed him in the hit *Stalag 17*. Strangely enough, Holden had not wanted to do either film. "Only actors who are ashamed to act are worth their salt," Wilder said of Holden. "He dies every time he has to act."

$\sim\bullet\sim$

"Bill was such a secret person," said Billy Wilder. "He would not open up—even with his close friends—or ask for help or at least someone to listen to him." Audrey was a listener. Bill was a man of contradictions—gregarious yet withdrawn; highly professional in his work yet determinedly nonchalant when talking about it. When he had first started, he wanted to be "the best motion picture actor in the world." Audrey shared a similar goal. They could tell each other everything.

Sabrina co-star Martha Hyer has recalled that Audrey and Bill "were together most evenings after shooting." To unwind and let off steam, they would have dinner at Lucy's El Adobe, a popular Mexican restaurant near the Paramount studios. One of the co-owners was Stephen Crane, no stranger to Hollywood relationships. He had once been married to Lana Turner and was the father of Lana's only child, Cheryl. Lucy's, a former speakeasy, was where many stars, producers, and directors from both Paramount and nearby RKO liked to go. The Spanish monastery–like facade had a certain charm, and the softly lit interior was warm and inviting. The bar was always bustling, the shop-talk and gossip nonstop. John Wayne, Robert Mitchum, Dick Powell, Ray Milland, and many others were among the regulars. Bill loved the ambiance; he felt comfortable there.

There were "hideaway" booths for those who wished to be discreet, and Holden was no stranger to them. But Bill and Audrey had nothing to hide—they were coworkers enjoying a meal together, talking about their movie and its problems. It was obvious to observers—among them, one evening, King Features Syndicate writer Alice Hughes—that their interest in each other was intense. Hughes recalled that you couldn't help but notice Hepburn and Holden. They had an aura about them. "They seemed unaware of their surroundings, totally absorbed in their conversation. Others were staring at them, of course, pretending not to, but they seemed oblivious."

They made each other laugh, as if their conversations were a most delightful game. When Audrey smiled, her face seemed to glow. Bill had a charismatic smile, too. Bogart had taken to referring to him as "Smiling Jim," a term Holden had applied to himself early in his career, a result of a series of vapid roles he'd had to play. After the very proper James Hanson, and the ultraserious Mel Ferrer, being with Bill had to be like escaping to the circus for Audrey.

The first to learn Audrey and Bill had become lovers was Ernest Lehman. Late one afternoon following the day's shooting, the belea-guered screenwriter entered Bill's dressing room without knocking, as was his habit, to drop off some scene changes. To his surprise, he found the two stars standing face-to-face, staring into each other's eyes with their hands clasped. Embarrassed, Lehman apologized and with-drew. He felt he had witnessed something deeply meaningful going on between them.

From that point, the news traveled fast. Nothing stayed a secret in Hollywood. But the public didn't know. As far as Paramount was concerned, if the chemistry between Hepburn and Holden was showing up on-screen, it was best to leave them alone for now (unlike MGM, where micromanaging actors' private lives was uppermost on the agenda). Besides, the front office knew never to interfere with a Billy Wilder picture, not while it stayed on budget. And the baroness, and Audrey's formidable new agent, Kurt Frings, knew it was best, at this juncture, to let Audrey be Audrey. She seemed happier than she had been in a long time. With Bill, she was able to relax her reserve. She felt like the young girl she was. She was able to laugh, to chatter and giggle. It was a relief not to have to be the regal Audrey. It happened fast, but she was not fighting it; she was falling in love.

For Bill, it had happened even faster. He was already in love. "Audrey was the love of my life," Holden said many years later, recalling: "Sometimes at night, I'd get a portable record player and we'd drive out to the country to a little clearing we'd found. We'd put on ballet music. Some of our most magic moments were there."

In Bill's eyes, Audrey was the ultimate prima ballerina. As he watched her dance, he was absorbed in her every expression, every gesture, every inflection of her being. And seeing this fascination, she responded to what she saw in his eyes. The scared little girl disappeared and a woman aware of her allure took her place. It happened in automatic response to his admiration. It was incredible—in Bill, Audrey had finally found the kind of loving audience for her dancing that she had sought all her life. If this wasn't heaven, it was close enough, for both of them. But he was married, and he continued to drink heavily.

Onetime Paramount publicist Teet Carle, who had worked with Holden in the early 1940s, kept in touch with friends on the lot and heard all about the Holden-Hepburn relationship. Carle, like Holden, had a drinking problem, and he wondered how young Audrey was reacting to that. As far as such things could be judged from the outside, it was not an issue for her; she took it in stride. If anything, Audrey appeared to have a calming influence on Bill.

Audrey had always told reporters that she was definitely not ready for marriage, and she'd meant it. But now, with Bill, she felt differently. Audrey and Bill, Bill and Audrey! Holden and Hepburn. It had a ring to it, she liked it. Loved it! Their chemistry together was undeniable, the attraction absolute. It was simple: he made her happy. He truly cared about her; the feeling was fervently mutual, and other practical considerations were simply blotted out.

Under the circumstances, the intrigue may have provided an additional soupçon of excitement for the lovers. Bill knew of far, out-of-the-way spots where they could dine, even dance, by candlelight; places where their romance could blossom unseen by jealous eyes and unhindered by the blinding glare of flashbulbs. Even the drives to these spots were romantic. He was affectionate, and she needed affection. Everything he did showed her that he cared; his every action was motivated by the need of receiving her love. They were both very demonstrative people, and the intimacy intoxicated both of them. They were fast approaching that point where reality and make-believe merge.

"That William Holden. Take a look at him," Bogie said poignantly to one of his longtime friends, Paramount producer A. C. Lyles, a visitor to the set one day. "You know, if I was as handsome as Bill Holden, I wouldn't have had any doubts why Bacall married me!" Many on the scene amused themselves by speculating about why Audrey had fallen in love with Bill. She had to know by now that there had been many other women. That was true, but Audrey was neither the first nor the last young woman in her twenties who felt that these problems were due solely to his unhappiness, which she could fix. Their love for each other would be the answer to everything.

⌒•⌒

Back on the set, Bogart had been complaining that Wilder was giving Audrey and Bill all the close-ups. Finally, in a scene with Holden, there would be close-ups of Bogie. Charles Lang spent hours supervising placement of the lights and camera, prompting one of the technicians to remark that it was more like preparation for a close-up of Greta Garbo, or Wilder's great pal Marlene Dietrich. At last, everything was set. Bogart was summoned, then walked to his marks. The makeup people did their final pat-downs, eliminating all shine on the actors' faces. All was ready to go. "Quiet on the set!" shouted AD "Charlie" Coleman.

"Action!" called Wilder. The dialogue began. As Bogart spoke his lines, Holden lit up a cigarette, hoping the smoke would make Bogie cough. "That fucking Holden over there, waving cigarettes around, crumpling paper, blowing smoke in my face. I want this sabotage ended!" shouted Bogart. The tension had to go somewhere. Wilder's back problems flared up, as the patient crew set up for a re-take. They'd have a juicy story to tell their families that evening.

Holden—who was known to have "liquid lunches"—had issues of his own. Martha Hyer, who played the role of Elizabeth Tyson in *Sabrina*, recalled that Holden sometimes drank so much that he had to rest until he sobered up, and the makeup people had to make adjustments and powder down the flush on his face. "One day," recalled Hyer, "Bill was very shaky, blowing his lines and not really in shape to work. Bogie quietly remarked, 'Methinks the lad hath partaken too much of the grape.'"

Holden lunged at him, and members of the crew acted quickly to pry them apart. It had been an ironic comment; between takes, according to Hyer, Bogie would often "ask for whiskey to be served in his dressing room," yet his drinking never seemed to interfere with his work.

Bogart's temper could, though. Throughout production there were constant schedule shifts. On one particular day, Wilder and Lehman had written a new version of that day's scene and were prepared to shoot it. When Bogart arrived, he discovered that Audrey and Bill already had copies of the revised pages. Somehow a copy had not been delivered to Bogart. He walked off the set, shutting down production. The hushed quiet, after his exit, was broken by a sudden peal of laughter from Audrey. Audrey later said she was often terrified of Bogart, but on this occasion his behavior meant she and Bill would have an unexpected free afternoon together. By now, the relationship had evolved into all-out passion.

Behind-the-scenes intrigue was not at all unusual in the course of motion picture production. On occasion, Audrey was a willing co-conspirator. Wilder, needing to rewrite certain scenes on the spot, secretly enlisted Audrey's aid. If she permitted him to say that she wasn't feeling well, the assistant director would have to call a break. She understood, and she cooperated. When this occurred during a scene with Bogart, he grumbled and retreated to his dressing room. And there was the time that Wilder returned with new script pages. Bogart read them over. After a long silence, he looked Wilder in the eye and asked him how old his daughter was.

"Seven," replied the director.

"Did she write this?" asked Bogart.

However, making all the actors shine brightly was in Wilder's best interest. Makeup people on the set were instructed to watch carefully during Bogart's scenes with Audrey; after a take, they needed to be very discreet in blotting the spittle off Audrey's face. Audrey never winced and, not wanting to embarrass the star, never brought it up. When their scenes were over, she got away from him as fast as she could, trying to avoid what he might come up with next.

When he felt Bogart was not behaving properly with Audrey or Wilder, Holden seethed. He considered himself Audrey's "guardian angel" and defender, and later said: "Most men who worked with her felt both fatherly or brotherly towards her, while harboring romantic feelings about her." Bogie harbored none of those feelings for young Hepburn. He had heard that Audrey had said that he "looked very nervous" during their love scenes. He took offense and began ridiculing her, imitating her voice and talking behind her back.

Veteran star Clifton Webb was a longtime friend of the Bogarts; Bogie and Bacall were staples at Webb's lavish parties. Webb asked Bogie how he enjoyed working with the industry's new dream girl, and he replied: "She's okay, if you like to do thirty-six takes." Bacall, who had recently starred with Marilyn Monroe in *How to Marry a Millionaire*, sympathized with her husband but asked what he was complaining about. In Marilyn's case, it was more like fifty takes, on a good day. Another time, Bogie described Audrey as a rank amateur who required at least ten takes. It was all grist for the gossip mill; the ultimate test would be the final picture. In the case of *Millionaire*, the film was a big hit, so all transgressions were forgiven. The tale was yet to be told on *Sabrina*.

It certainly showed promise, because for all the turmoil on the set, magic was happening on film. There was a brief scene between Bogart and Holden—the two brothers encounter each other in the early morning, as Bogart, sartorially perfect in suit, tie, and hat, is heading for his limousine and a hard day at the office. Holden, disheveled and hung over, is returning from a night out on the town. Holden mocks his brother's devotion to work, exclaiming, with bravado, how ridiculous it is to go to the office on a Sunday!

"Today is Wednesday," replies Bogart with exactly the right bite, his timing impeccable. And Wilder's sense of humor hadn't deserted him: he wrote a line of dialogue for Bogart in which, while riding to the office in a limo and dictating the day's schedule for his secretary, he instructs her, "And get me tickets for *The Seven Year Itch*." It was a current Broadway hit slated to be Wilder's next movie, for 20th Century-Fox.

There was the memorable scene with Audrey and Bogie in the sports car, where she sings "La Vie en Rose," and he asks her to sing it again, obviously Wilder's homage to the classic *Casablanca* moment when a lovesick Rick asks Dooley Wilson, "Play it again, Sam. . . ." As he's driving the sports car, staring straight ahead with Sabrina by his side, Linus says with exactly the right emotion: "If I was ten years younger. . . ."

Meanwhile, Bill's impassioned feelings for Audrey had reached yet another level, and Audrey's nerves almost got the best of her when, late one afternoon, Bill brightly announced: "Ardis wants to meet you."

Chapter

4

S HE LOOKED LIKE A BEAUTIFUL BUT OLDER AUDREY.

Ardis Ankerson was her birth name, and from the beginning she insisted that Bill and their friends call her Ardis, not Brenda, her stage name. Friends included Ronald Reagan and Nancy Davis, to whom Bill and Ardis served as best man and matron of honor at the Reagans' wedding, on March 4, 1952. Reagan was grateful to Ardis: "She had arranged for a cake at their home, and a photographer, so we'd have wedding pictures." No reporters were on hand. Reagan didn't want them around; he had been burned by the negative coverage during his divorce from actress Jane Wyman.

That was fine with the Holdens, who were wary of the press as well. Ardis was no stranger to publicity; she'd had plenty of it during her days as a working actress. She was a gorgeous, Philippines-born brunette, three years older than Bill, and had been anxious to succeed in her career. Errol Flynn, no less, had been her leading man in two films, *The Sea Hawk* and *Footsteps in the Dark*. Ultimately, none of the ten movies she had made by the time she met and married Bill, in 1941, had made her a star. But who was to say that it wouldn't have happened if she had ever gotten the "right" role.

Ardis had left her husband, actor Richard Gaines, to marry Bill, who adopted the former couple's five-year-old daughter, Virginia. Husband and wife were both strong personalities, and tensions and undercurrents in their relationship led to a tacit understanding that suited both of them. Contrary to popular perception, Ardis was not the little woman warming her hands by the fire while waiting for her errant husband to come home (which he invariably did). In fact, she had a roving eye herself. Obviously, the Holdens were comfortable with their open lifestyle, but they were always souls of discretion. They had to be; any actor's career would have suffered a crippling blow during those days when morals clauses were still written into studio contracts.

Interestingly, Ardis was not one to bask in reflected glory. She often had something to say that would bring Bill down a peg or two if people's compliments—about his looks, his talent, and so on—got out of hand. Nor was she reluctant to disagree with him. If, for example, Bill said he thought an actor's performance in a film was lousy and she thought otherwise, Ardis would reply: "Oh, I thought he was wonderful in it."

Ardis was not unaware, and not surprised, that her husband had a crush on Audrey Hepburn. Of all the women he had been involved with up to this point, there had been two serious relationships: actress Gail Russell, an ethereally beautiful brunette, nine years younger than Ardis, under contract to Paramount; she was a highly neurotic young woman who drank to control her nerves. Men—Bill and John Wayne among them—wanted to protect and help her. Heartthrob Guy Madison married her, but sadly, her alcoholism was an eventual death sentence.

Blonde Diana Lynn, another Paramount contractee, eleven years younger than Ardis, was Bill's other serious extramarital partner. The less serious flings included one with Shelley Winters, who bragged in later years that she and Bill had enjoyed an annual sexual rendezvous across nearly a decade; at one point he gave her a beautiful diamond watch, which she kept all of her life.

In 1969, in New York City, when Shelley, a nonstop talker, was in charge of an Actors Studio benefit premiere of Bob Fosse's film *Sweet Charity*, she told the Universal studio publicist that she'd heard Bill Holden was in town. "I'd invite him to the opening, but I haven't seen him in years and we didn't part on the best of terms. Will you guys call him and invite him?" Holden declined the invitation.

At the time Bill fell in love with Audrey, the Holdens' two sons were ages seven and ten. It speaks well of Bill and Ardis that the boys later said that they had no feelings of having lived an unhappy childhood. In fact, they regarded it as a special one. Bill was caring and loving, and seemed a child himself when he played with them and their toys. Whether he'd been drinking or not, as far as Scott and Peter were concerned, Dad was always in a good mood and lots of fun.

❧

Audrey was no coward. Of course she would meet Bill's wife. It was the civilized thing to do. Then she had second thoughts. Outwardly, she was a vision of confidence. Her insides, however, were churning. What had Bill gotten her into? This could be the kind of "scene" she had seen in women's movies from the old Hollywood days, a confrontation between wife and—was it possible? Was she actually playing the real-life role of a home wrecker?

Audrey had been emphatic with Bill—marriage or nothing. Audrey wanted children. He understood; there wasn't a moment's hesitation in Bill's reply. He was going to ask Ardis for a divorce.

Always socially adept, Audrey was reduced to near-adolescent hysteria at the prospect of meeting Bill's wife. How much did Ardis really know? What had Bill told her? In European society, situations like these were not uncommon; it was natural that Audrey was highly curious about the woman Bill had stayed married to for a dozen years. The drive to the Holden domicile, which was nestled in Toluca Lake, a San Fernando Valley enclave, seemed interminable. It would have been so easy to tell the driver, "Turn back! Take me home!" But she did not.

The Holden home wasn't in a particularly fashionable location as far as Hollywood's A-list was concerned. Designed by noted architect Paul Williams, the house was a Georgian-style, flagstone-clad, two-story affair, modest by movie-star standards. Nonetheless, it was a stark contrast to Audrey's tiny apartment (most actresses in her superstar-on-the-rise position would have demanded, and received, a palatial residence to live in while making a film). As Audrey drove up to the entrance—not a long, winding driveway, but a simple, short walk from the curb to the front door—she took a deep breath and steeled herself for what was certain to be a difficult evening. She realized, for the first time, that this was Bill's home, and this woman she was about to meet was his wife, the mother of his two children. All that had never seemed real to her before.

The inside of the house was warm and welcoming—pure Americana, bright colors, and traditional furniture. Comfort, not opulence, was the keynote. The bar area featured framed stills from Bill's films, including solo shots of Barbara Stanwyck and Dorothy Lamour.

When Audrey saw Ardis, she was impressed. The woman was beautiful; the role of injured wife did not suit her. But the beautiful Ardis brought out the competitive spirit in Audrey. Hepburn held her head high, gave out one of her killer smiles, and said: "Oh, I'm so happy to meet you."

Ardis's heart must have frozen at the sight of her—here was this radiant creature, fifteen years younger than she, who wasn't merely beautiful but had unique qualities of class and an almost spiritual grace. The others Bill had brought home were beautiful, but not like this; this was not someone Ardis could have been prepared for. Unlike many Hollywood beauties away from the camera, Audrey even had a beautiful speaking voice! There was nothing strident or uncultured in this package. She was a wife's worst nightmare, and to compound matters, she seemed like a nice person!

Over the course of the evening Ardis observed that there was much more going on than had been the case with Bill's other entanglements. From the way Bill was looking at Audrey, Ardis realized that she was no passing fancy. Mrs. Holden was scared. Lately, Bill had been drinking more than ever and seemed unable to stop. He wasn't yet a wealthy man, but that goal was in sight; was he actually willing to let it all slip through his fingers for Audrey Hepburn? Ardis didn't put it past him. As soon as Audrey left, the gloves came off and Ardis went into attack mode. She demanded that Bill stop seeing that woman.

Ironically, at the time there were photo layouts of the "Happy Holdens" in major national magazines—"Bill, Brenda, and their boys enjoying a cozy evening at home," "Bill and Brenda enjoying a movie in their den. . . ." The image makers had been very thorough.

∼•∽

That awful evening was over, but Audrey and Bill's affair wasn't. Their ongoing passion proved that defiance was a potent aphrodisiac. For Bill, as well as Audrey, being in love made all the difference. His marriage was emotionally over, and his mind was made up. He *was* going to divorce Ardis and marry Audrey. It seemed like the most natural next step, and he popped the question. She accepted. By this time Audrey had moved from her apartment at 3435 Wilshire Boulevard to a two-room rental at 10368 Wilshire. Their trysts continued there, and in their dressing rooms.

One day, Audrey was having difficulty with her dialogue in a scene with Bogart and Holden. "Maybe you should stay home and study your lines instead of going out every night," Bogart said, grinning wickedly. Stony silence on the sidelines. "Okay, ladies and gentlemen," shouted Wilder, in a voice even louder than usual, standing alongside the camera. "Again please!"

$\sim\!\cdot\!\sim$

A welcome reprieve: Audrey, Bill, and Bogie were excited that they would be going to New York for location shooting. The trip, meticulously planned by the studio, would be platinum-class all the way: the best hotels, chauffeured limos around the clock, plus a small army of production people, publicists, and security on hand to insure all ran smoothly.

Scenes would be shot at estates on Long Island, and in and around Manhattan, including Wall Street. Photos of Audrey and Bill together, on the streets of New York, subsequently appeared in newspapers and magazines throughout the world. Hepburn, her usual Vogue-incarnate self, was in her element. For one scene, she was dressed casually in a black, long-sleeve, turtleneck pullover and capri pants, black ballet slippers completing the timelessly chic ensemble. For another, she wore a dramatic black suit, hat, and low-heeled black pumps. Bill was always in suit, tie, and hat—the hat sometimes worn at a jaunty angle, Sinatra-style. Because he was a head taller, Bill always gazed down lovingly at Audrey, and she adored that.

Gaping crowds gathered behind ropes to watch the filming, standing in line hoping for autographs between setups. The stars created a sensation wherever they went—it took only seconds for everyone to know they were there. There were no photographers or crowds to contend with, of course, when Audrey and Bill were alone in their trailers or hotel suites. Bernard Serlin, an advertising-publicity man working for Warner Bros., was in the Wall Street area during filming and dropped by to say hello to a friend, a studio photographer. No newcomer to the film business, Serlin was familiar with the behavior of temperamental stars and was surprised at the happy, nonstop interplay between Hepburn and Holden off-camera. "They were like two high school kids in love," he said. "I asked my friend if they were like that all the time. He smiled and said, 'All the time.'"

New York–based syndicated columnist Earl Wilson had spies in the best restaurants, hotels, and elsewhere all over town. His West Coast sources had tipped him off on what was going on between Audrey and Bill. In fact, he had been following her exploits since the James Hanson days. Wilson, a physically small man from the Midwest with a soft-spoken manner, was a bird dog when it came to tracking down a story. He contacted Paramount's New York press reps, pressing them for further information. "It's news to us," was their reply. Wilson called his press contacts at other studios' New York offices. Paul Kamey, at Universal, told Wilson that he had heard from Paramount pals on the West Coast that Audrey and Bill were "carrying on," but there were no specifics; and Kamey was speaking off the record. Wilson was not going to stake his reputation on information that could not be verified. What a coup, though, if he could scoop Hollywood-based rivals Hedda, Louella, and Sheilah.

Audrey and Bill had been lucky so far. She would be harmed far more than Holden if their affair became public. The public was more understanding when it came to men. Only a couple of years earlier, Ava Gardner had been vilified for "luring" Frank Sinatra into leaving wife and family to marry her (in fact, it was Sinatra who had pursued Ava).

But Ava was a sex symbol, and it went with the territory. Audrey was Cinderella and would not be forgiven so easily, if at all. The press would sweep down on her like the proverbial swarm of locusts.

Bogart, meanwhile, was on good behavior in New York. One day, he and Audrey were filming outdoors near Long Island Sound. A sailor whose prized possession was his yacht, *Santana,* Bogie was always happiest near or on the water. "An actor needs something to stabilize his personality, something to nail down what he really is, not what he is currently pretending to be," he once observed. Pretending to be "Linus Larabee" was taking its toll; it wasn't pleasant to know people were referring to him as having the personality of a razor blade. This day's scene was a crucial one between Linus and Sabrina. Between takes, Audrey said she was chilly. Bogie took off his jacket and put it around her shoulders. He could be a charmer when he wanted to.

During the New York shoot, Bogie dropped in at Toots Shor's restaurant and enjoyed a rare evening out on the town at another of his favorite haunts. "I met him at El Morocco [a top nightclub, frequented by stars and café society notables], and thought he was the sexiest man alive," recalled Texas-born showgirl Pat Gaston, a gorgeous, statuesque blonde close to Audrey's age, who was soon to marry playboy millionaire Tommy Manville. "Bogart was a total gentleman, not anything like the tough character he was on-screen. I thought there was something very vulnerable about him—the expression in his eyes, his demeanor. You wanted to put your arms around him and say, 'Don't worry, honey, everything's going to be okay.'"

The "grace period" in New York couldn't last forever. Back at the studio, Bogart began calling Wilder "a Kraut bastard" and "Nazi," despite the fact that Wilder had lost members of his family in the Holocaust. And, of course, Bogie's beloved Betty was Jewish. He also mimicked

Wilder's thick German accent, sometimes responding to his direction with a perfect Erich von Stroheim–like "*Ja-wohl!*"

Audrey's smile slowly faded on these occasions. Shooting, fortunately, was drawing to a close; it was a miracle the film was getting finished.

Portrait sessions in the studio's photo galleries were less enervating—no dialogue to be memorized. Shots of the stars were taken to be used for advertising, publicizing, and promoting the film. Stylists and makeup people were present, working feverishly, as all photo combinations were covered: Audrey and Bogart together; Audrey and Bill together; Bill and Bogart together; all three of them together. The Richard Avedon–type session—shoot fast, get spontaneous reactions, set up unexpected situations—was an approach that hadn't quite yet infiltrated the mainstream.

Audrey was totally comfortable in this milieu; formal photographs were never a problem. In her solo sessions, she was a photographer's dream, and so were the photos; noted freelance photographer Bob Willoughby's images were timeless, and he was greatly impressed by her expertise at taking direction, her ability to concentrate and focus on making sure that everything was just right.

One would have assumed, seeing Audrey interact with Bogie, that she adored him. In the photos with Bill, her joy shines through—Audrey reclining, with Bill hovering over her; the couple staring at each other, blissful expressions on their faces; then, very close together, so the camera could catch them both in extreme close-up. The setups took a long time to light and shoot; it was an intensely intimate, enjoyable experience for the pair.

It wasn't Ardis, the studio, their agents, or advisers who ended Audrey and Bill's affair. It had lasted through the filming of *Sabrina*, but those blissful months would end with a devastating revelation. Those close to her knew that she was deeply in love. The couple shared an emotional intimacy that precluded words. One smile from him and she knew she was understood, and valued, and cared for. She would never believe he had a shadow side.

Often, during their relationship, Audrey spoke of children. She told him she wanted three, maybe four, and would retire from the screen to raise them. Once, while chattering brightly about the names of their future children, suddenly an embarrassed smile, tinged with fear, crept into Bill's face.

What did it mean? He told her that the one thing, the only thing they could not have together—was children. He would recall the fixed expression in her eyes; how she stood looking at him like a hurt, bewildered child. Her eyes searched his face as he explained that he'd had a vasectomy years earlier at Ardis's urging, and it could not be reversed. He was physically unable to have any more children.

He waited until now to tell her this? Her sudden formal, remote air on hearing this kept Bill at arm's length. He hoped she wouldn't hate him. It had to have made them both sad to know that the trusting, simple part of their relationship was gone for good, certainly as far as she was concerned. Bill, however, never gave up hope that some miracle would set things straight. She ended the affair on the spot, but they were hardly out of each other's lives.

Chapter

5

TWO MONTHS BEFORE, EVERYTHING HAD BEEN SO DIFFERENT— she had been happy with Bill, and she missed him. She still loved him and thought of him often—the smiles, the laughter, the kisses. But it was over now. She was alone. At this vulnerable moment, Mel Ferrer reappeared. Audrey was happy to see him. Mel had news: he was now a free man. In the months since they had met, he had divorced his wife. His attentiveness and sense of romantic urgency was just the antidote to Bill that Audrey required.

Bill's antidote to Audrey was about to enter his life. He undoubtedly hoped her appearance on the scene, and his subsequent involvement with her, would make Audrey jealous and sorry that she had abandoned him; then she would want to bring him back into her life. Holden did not give up easily. Actor Glenn Ford noted that his friend Bill was not a man who liked to lose, and he never accepted failure without a fight.

Mel convinced Audrey that he loved her and would dedicate himself to her as a woman and an artist, and although he had four children already, he was eager to have more with her. Now that she had a perspective on their relationship, she felt a sense of guilt on the effect her affair with Bill might have had on his children; she hoped they hadn't been hurt the way she had been by her own mother's love affairs and divorces.

Mel's background spoke well of him. His father was a well-known Cuban American surgeon; his mother was socially prominent. His sisters and nephew worked for *Newsweek* magazine. Everything about him seemed first-rate. Of course, he had a past. So did she. Mel and Audrey had much in common on all levels, going back to their childhoods—Audrey had experienced malnutrition during her youth, Mel had had to contend with a bout of polio. They were both survivors.

Ferrer was no Bill Holden—he did not have that beguiling, devil-may-care attitude; he was not as devastatingly attractive or sensitive. The very lack of those qualities, perhaps, which had so overwhelmed Audrey, was a plus at this juncture. There was nothing boyishly playful about Mel. He outlined a wonderfully rosy future for Audrey and himself—working together, loving together—they could be the successors to Alfred Lunt and Lynn Fontanne, to Laurence Olivier and Vivien Leigh. He even had a play, *Ondine*, ready to go that the two of them could star in on Broadway. He had told her about it when they first met. And there was fresh news: Alfred Lunt said he would direct! Was she interested now? Yes!

There was no question in the public's mind that Audrey could successfully fulfill the female half of a Lunt-Fontanne, Olivier-Leigh equation; with laserlike determination, Mel was intent on proving that he was Audrey's worthy equal on the world stage. She liked the idea.

In the meantime, the Audrey-and-Bill saga had to be brought to an acceptable conclusion. Too many people knew about it. There could still be scandal and repercussions. A bizarre scenario was about to be played out, starring Audrey, Bill, Ardis, and Mel. The Holden home was the setting for an announcement. Present were the four principals—along with key Paramount and select other executives involved with Audrey's and Bill's careers.

"Bill and Mel were as 'friendly' that night as two lions ready to tear each other's throats out," recalled a top-level Paramount (later MCA) executive present on the occasion. "And a scalpel was necessary to cut through the tension between Audrey and Ardis. It was quite a night!" The studio wanted nothing to tarnish Audrey or Bill's images, or the prospects for *Sabrina*, which had been previewed successfully, even minus final soundtrack and other effects, and was expected to be a big hit on its release later in the year.

The purpose of that night's gathering was to announce Audrey's engagement to Mel—a move intended to diffuse all the innuendo and gossip that had been building for months about Audrey and Bill. By having Audrey announce her betrothal at Bill's house, with Bill's wife present—how could anyone say there had been anything serious to all those nasty rumors? Cocktails were abundant, conversation was forced; a synthetic cordiality filled the room. Audrey's eyes avoided Bill's. His bloodshot eyes underscored his angst. He was clearly a man carrying a torch.

Audrey's fans were delighted to learn that their idol was engaged. It seemed she had found true love at last, although Mel Ferrer was hardly the kind of romantic figure the fan magazines could get excited about. And to insiders there remained the question: Were Audrey and Bill really no longer a couple? All knew how mercurial and unpredictable actors were when it came to matters of the heart.

The Oscars were coming up—March 25, 1954, was the big night, and insiders eagerly anticipated the drama that might be in store: Audrey and Bill, face-to-face, sweating out the Oscar derby. Audrey, however, wouldn't be there; she would not have to see or interact with Bill. She was in New York, starring on Broadway, opposite Mel Ferrer in *Ondine,* in which she portrayed the title character, a water sprite.

Director Alfred Lunt had succumbed to the Hepburn magic: "While most people simply have nice manners, Audrey has authentic charm and class." And the estimable Mr. Lunt had plenty of superstar friends to compare her with.

But she had not expected the play to be such an ordeal, and the theater community was abuzz over Mel's supposed unwillingness to permit Audrey to take a solo curtain call. Mel was labeled a Svengali; Audrey his bewitched Trilby. "It was the talk of the town," recalled wire service correspondent Doug Anderson. Others noted that it was ironic that although Ferrer was portraying a knight errant in the play, when it came to taking bows, obviously chivalry was dead.

Oscar fever was at a high pitch, even in New York, because the ceremonies would be televised from both coasts this year, with several major nominees in New York, including Audrey, Deborah Kerr, Geraldine Page, and Thelma Ritter. Hepburn, the girl who said she couldn't deal with too many emotions at once, was beside herself when the evening arrived. Photographers surrounded her from the moment she left her show and got into a limousine, complete with police escort, sirens screaming, to race her to the Oscar ceremonies at New York's NBC Century Theater.

En route, she removed her blonde stage wig and, once at the Century, went to a dressing room to remove her heavy stage makeup. A *Life* magazine photographer had been given permission to "follow" Audrey, but other photographers weren't shy about doing their jobs, trying to coax her out of the dressing room: "Hey, Skinny, come on out!"

The baroness was waiting for her daughter inside the packed theater, which was crowded and noisy. "Smile, dear," said her mother, as Audrey sat down. Gary Cooper, on film (he was in Mexico) was reading the list of nominees for Best Actress. Donald O'Connor, hosting the Academy Awards in Hollywood (Fredric March was the New York emcee) opened the envelope and shouted out Audrey's name.

The applause was loud and sustained. One account related Audrey's reaction: "A very confused young lady mounted the steps to the stage, turned suddenly, and began to wander off toward the wings. Fredric March guided the winner back to the podium. 'This is too much,' Audrey sighed."

Holden, with a smiling, formally gowned Ardis by his side, was in Hollywood when Shirley Booth in New York (she was the previous year's Best Actress winner, for *Come Back, Little Sheba*) announced the Best Actor winner: "William Holden!"

Afterward, when asked how she was going to celebrate, Audrey said: "At home, with Mother." However, after an hour with Mother, Audrey and Mel joined Deborah Kerr, and her husband, Anthony Bartley, for post-awards cocktails at the Plaza Hotel's elegant nightclub, the Persian Room. Many of New York's leading columnists were already there, including Dorothy Kilgallen and her husband, producer Dick Kollmar, along with Leonard Lyons, Louis Sobol, and Earl Wilson. The public might have been kept unaware of Audrey's romance with Bill Holden, but it was common knowledge to the showbiz press. Kilgallen's eagle eye was alert to anything signaling trouble in paradise between Audrey and Mel, but there was no such news to report. The young star seemed content and affectionate with him.

Holden's post-Oscar celebration took place at Romanoff's, the restaurant frequented by the town's leading stars and filmmakers, where Bill toasted Billy Wilder: "Of course, I knew it all the time." But there would be no photographs that night of Hepburn and Holden together, clutching each other and their Oscars.

The morning after, Audrey met with the press in New York, wearing the perfect black suit—V-neck, long-sleeved fitted jacket, pencil skirt, black pumps, perfectly scaled hoop earrings, her hair short with bangs. She posed, as she was asked to, sitting pinup-girl style on the floor, Oscar alongside her; in each hand she held up batches of congratulatory telegrams. A huge smile lit up her face. She couldn't wait until the photographers left, so she could light up a cigarette.

Several days later, another contest was decided: Audrey and her friend Deborah Kerr had been nominated for the Tony for Best Leading Actress in a Play; Audrey for *Ondine* and Kerr for *Tea and Sympathy*. The prize went to Audrey. *New York Times* critic Brooks Atkinson had described Hepburn's performance as "tremulously lovely," and theater historian Philip G. Hill wrote that the show was "a work of extraordinary beauty." Alfred Lunt won the Tony for Best Director that year. Mel, alas, was Tony-less.

~•~

Bill was desperate to win Audrey back. When she returned to Hollywood, there was an awkward meeting between them when both posed, clutching their respective Oscars but not each other, in front of a giant poster for *Sabrina*.

Holden was soon off to the Far East to begin shooting his next picture, *The Bridges at Toko-Ri*, based on the James Michener novel. Bill had formulated a perverse plan to show Audrey how hurt he was; he hoped that after recognizing his torment, she would want to bring him back into her life. "So I set out around the world with the idea of screwing a woman in every country I visited. My plan succeeded, though sometimes with difficulty." When he later encountered Audrey at Paramount, he told her what he had done. "You know what she said? 'Oh, Bill!' That's all. 'Oh, Bill!' Just as though I were some naughty boy. What a waste!"

◄ The public was never the wiser: Bogart actively disliked both his co-stars.

Courtesy Photofest

▼ Holden and Bogart. They did not like each other.

Courtesy Photofest

▲ Bill, Audrey, and Billy Wilder watch *Sabrina* rushes in the screening room. Neither Bill nor Audrey was confident, then or later, about their work. Wilder said the most talented actors rarely thought they were any good.

Courtesy Photofest

◄ ► Filming, with Bill, on *Sabrina* location in New York City. It was a happy time for the couple.

Courtesy Everett Collection

Courtesy Everett Collection

◄ ▲ The emotions were real.

Courtesy Photofest

▶ Givenchy adjusts a scarf on Audrey during a fitting (1958). She was his muse.

Courtesy AP Images

▼ Audrey in *Sabrina* black, timelessly stylish. "All women who have it [style] share one thing: originality," noted Diana Vreeland. Audrey's "look" emerged at exactly the right moment in her career.

Courtesy Photofest

▲ Bill with wife, Ardis, at Romanoff's restaurant, holding his Oscar for *Stalag 17*.

Courtesy Photofest

◀ Arriving solo, on March 25, 1954, for the 1953 Oscar ceremonies in New York. Audrey was appearing on the Broadway stage in *Ondine*. Bill was on the west coast, attending the festivities with his wife.

Courtesy Photofest

▲ Back on the west coast, Audrey poses with Bill and her Oscar, a giant poster for *Sabrina* behind them. She had ended their affair.

Courtesy Photofest

He still held out hope, in spite of what Audrey did next: she married Mel Ferrer. Bill never thought she would go through with it. But the ceremony took place on September 24, 1954, in Bürgenstock, Switzerland. Audrey looked spectacular in a white, tea-length, bouffant-sleeved, princesslike Givenchy masterpiece, a circle of flowers atop her beautifully coiffed head. The marriage was not merely movie star news; it was a fashion event, as her wedding dress reinforced a trend: the short bridal gown. Mel looked very serious, gazing intently at Audrey with a smile on his face.

Bill could not avoid the news, or the photographs, which appeared in major newspapers and magazines throughout the world. Even television news covered the event. "Accept it, live with it, get on with your life" was advice any close friend or therapist would have given Bill (indeed, may have given him). But that wasn't how Bill lived his life. He never made strangers of his emotions. His heart was broken, the pain was real, and it was deep. And so he indulged himself in a world-class bender.

Bill's new leading lady was certainly a distraction. She was an actress Audrey was well aware of, and was often compared to: ravishing, blonde Grace Kelly. Her star had risen almost as fast as Audrey's. She was borrowed from MGM to portray Bill's wife in *The Bridges at Toko-Ri*.

Paramount released *Sabrina* during this period and hit the jackpot—the year's Best Actor and Best Actress Oscar winners, together with Oscar-winner Bogart, were all in the same picture. And it was directed by yet another Oscar winner, one of the few directors whose name the public knew. Billy Wilder's final Paramount picture was a hit. Audrey proved *Roman Holiday* hadn't been a fluke, and her star status was assured. Her image as the screen's adult Cinderella would endure indefinitely, even though Sabrina was one of her last Cinderella roles. Both on-screen and in her private life after Holden, Cinderella was entering a new phase. *Sabrina* had catapulted her to top-rank leading lady. From here on, she was granted the ultimate perquisite for a film actor: script approval. Bill's unconditional love and support had certainly been a vital element in enabling her to create a memorable characterization of Sabrina.

Arguably, it was Bogart who had scored a coup. Cary Grant would have been great, but considering the role, the results risked being predictable. Coming from Bogart, the performance was a delightful surprise, and critics sang his praises. The actor apologized to Wilder for his behavior, saying that personal issues away from the set were responsible. All was forgiven ("Success is the best deodorant," as Elizabeth Taylor once observed). Wilder later said, after Bogart died, "[He] always wanted to play the hero. In the end, he was."

Bill's "effortless" performance maintained his status as a quintessential leading man. In the industry Holden became known as "Golden Holden," with a string of smash-hit pictures on the horizon. His feelings for Audrey remained constant; his hopes for a future with her remained alive. They would work together again, and be together again.

Chapter

6

B ILL'S ANTIDOTE TO AUDREY HAD BEEN LABELED AN "ICY beauty" by the press, but in reality Grace Kelly was red hot. If, as Bill hoped, Audrey suffered pangs of jealousy and resentment envisioning "her Bill" with the beautiful Grace, she had good cause.

Toko-Ri producer William Perlberg had been delighted to see how well Bill and Grace looked together. Grace had seen Holden's movies, and he had seen hers. Neither was disappointed by their initial face-to-face contact, and they would be totally believable as husband and wife. Chemistry was vital—producers and directors hoped for and encouraged it. It was in everybody's best interest to capture real feelings on film.

Kelly's scenes with Holden were filmed in Hollywood around the time Audrey got married. Prince Rainier and Monaco were two years off, but in the meantime, Grace was emerging as Audrey's rival both as a respected actress and a worldwide icon of style and beauty. In addition to Bill Holden, it is fascinating how much the two women had in common. Both Audrey and Grace were leading adventurous private lives, mostly under the radar. Thanks to masterful career management and an aura of class that was all their own, their ladylike images were remaining intact. Both Audrey and Grace were very different from their on-screen personas. "Grace wasn't shy," said her sister Peggy. "She was just quiet." The same could have been said of Audrey. And just as Audrey didn't like certain aspects of her own looks, Grace had similar reservations about herself. She was self-conscious about what she considered her big jaw and told friends that she never *felt* beautiful.

"I found it interesting that there was definitely a cultural difference between them," noted MCA executive Taft Schreiber, who was also a renowned art collector. "Grace, in every way, was an All-American girl, while Audrey was pure European. Both were soft-spoken, but you knew Audrey was to-the-manor-born. So was Grace, but it was a different manor."

Pamela Mason, wife of British actor James Mason, was always outspoken on the subject of Hollywood's beauties, especially newcomers like Hepburn and Kelly. As far as Mrs. Mason was concerned, nuances of breeding and beauty aside, Audrey and Grace shared a common characteristic with other stars: "All of them had physically large heads," she said. "The men, too. If you went to a nightclub, or a screening, you saw them right away, no matter where they were sitting. They stood out because their heads were larger, literally, than other people's. That's why the camera singled them out."

Be that as it may, Audrey and Grace represented a turning point in the public's tastes. Kelly, like Hepburn, was the antithesis of a "typical" Hollywood actress. She, too, came from a privileged background but had been a rebel in a wealthy, suffocating, Kennedy-like family. Her uncle, George Kelly, was a noted playwright; he'd written the Pulitzer Prize–winning *Craig's Wife*. A friend of Grace's family claimed that the "high-powered friends" of Grace's father "got Grace going in acting; she didn't just rise to success." But Grace had indeed paid her acting dues; she had spent years in the theater and had done yeoman work on live television—she was even a judge at an annual Miss America pageant and had been a successful model.

Both were born the same year (Audrey was six months older), and both were defining their generation and would influence succeeding ones. Even the career parallels are fascinating: whereas Audrey had had Gregory Peck as her first important leading man, Grace had Gary Cooper in *High Noon,* followed by Clark Gable in *Mogambo* (for which she had recently been in contention for an Oscar as Best Supporting Actress). Grace and Gable became lovers, and she was hoping to marry him, but he told her he was too old for her at age fifty-two. PR executive Marion Billings, then a receptionist at MGM, recalled Grace crying her eyes out at this turn of events. But Kelly and Gable remained friends, and he was her escort at the Oscars.

Audrey had William Wyler as her director-mentor, and Grace had the equally well regarded John Ford, as well as Alfred Hitchcock. *Dial M for Murder* and *Rear Window* were awaiting release as she filmed *The Bridges at Toko-Ri.* Grace supposedly wanted to marry Ray Milland, her forty-seven-year-old *Dial M for Murder* co-star, who was already married with children. Keeping Grace's love life under wraps kept the studio very busy. (And Paramount was worried about fallout from Audrey's private life?) Whereas Audrey had just co-starred with Bogart and Holden, Grace was about to star opposite Holden in two films, and then with Cary Grant.

Audrey and Grace were new kinds of sex symbols. "Hollywood amuses me," said Grace. "Holier-than-thou for the public and unholier-than-the-devil in reality." Audrey, while aware she was hardly a "conventional" sex goddess, knew she had sex appeal. "It doesn't stand out a mile, but it's there." Kelly's face was the physically perfect one; Hepburn was not conventionally beautiful, but she was perfect in her imperfections. They appealed to exactly the same audience—and obviously to Bill Holden.

Grace, of course, had heard all about Bill and Audrey—who in town hadn't? One can imagine Audrey's reaction, and those in her inner circle, on reading in official material Paramount distributed to the press the following quote from Bill: "Grace has the faculty of reminding me of my own wife. Women like Grace Kelly and Audrey Hepburn help us to believe in the innate dignity of man."

"Can you imagine the mileage we'd get out of a shot of the three of them together?" This was suggested during a meeting of the Paramount publicity department, when a veteran studio publicist proposed that at some point they try to arrange to have a photo taken of the trio—Audrey and Grace, with Bill in the middle—with credits to all the films they had coming out. It would be a shot that would be picked up by every wire service in town and circulated around the world. After the laughter died down, a voice spoke up and said it was a great idea and would be arranged just as soon as a family of pigs flew over the Paramount lot.

～•～

Kelly hadn't wanted to do *Bridges at Toko-Ri* at first; hers was too small a role. But it was an important one, and, as Kelly's MCA agents pointed out, a very smart career move to have Bill Holden as her leading man. MGM agreed to the loan-out.

Grace had just stopped seeing Ray Milland, reportedly because of a plea from actress Ann Sothern, a close friend of Milland's wife, Mal. Sothern wrote to Grace, in a hand-delivered letter, that she would be wrecking the life "of a very wonderful woman." However, one of Grace's closest friends, the beautiful, dark-haired actress Rita Gam, who had made a movie with Milland, said she never got the impression that Grace was much interested in him, and perhaps Sothern's letter provided her with the excuse to move on.

Gossip regarding Grace and Bill didn't take long to circulate, requiring a statement from Grace's sister, Lizanne Kelly, which inadvertently confirmed the rumors: "If a lovely girl and a handsome fellow have to 'play' at being husband and wife all day, they're bound to have problems switching off when the show is over."

The Bill-and-Grace show was hardly over, even though when *Bridges at Toko-Ri* wrapped, Grace flew back to New York and Bill resumed his life with Ardis. Still, there were always reminders of Audrey. When the Holdens flew to Rome, where Bill was to receive an award as Best Foreign Actor for *Sabrina,* there was a screening of the film. Watching himself with Audrey was a bittersweet experience. It was hard to salvage a broken heart, but Grace Kelly had managed to stop the bleeding—her irrepressible laugh took the edge off things.

Starting a new film would keep Bill occupied. He was set to star with Jennifer Jones and Bing Crosby in *The Country Girl,* a film version of the hit Broadway play by Clifford Odets (whose *Golden Boy* had launched Bill to stardom). It was a powerful drama of life in the theater. When the originally cast Jennifer Jones revealed to producer William Perlberg and director George Seaton that she was pregnant, it was crisis time. Jones's husband, *Gone with the Wind* producer David O. Selznick, implored the producers to proceed. If they began production right away, it wouldn't be a problem; Jennifer's pregnancy wouldn't show for many weeks. That pregnancy provided the ultimate career boost for Grace Kelly, who got the part. At first, MGM had refused to okay another loan-out for their hot property. After a conversation between Lew Wasserman, Grace's agent, and MGM's Ben Thau, the studio agreed to the deal.

The cast change was, of course, fine with Holden. The shooting schedule would be three months, not the whirlwind of *Bridges at Toko-Ri* and the mere three weeks it took to film his scenes with Grace. Bill would have a lot more time to get to know Grace better. But Bing Crosby, who was still one of Paramount's biggest stars, balked, complaining that Kelly didn't have the experience to take on such a difficult role. Jennifer Jones was an Oscar winner who had been a top star for over a decade and was ten years older than Grace.

The producers were aware of the real reason for Crosby's objections to Grace: a budding personal relationship between them had fizzled out, and Crosby had no desire or intention to reward her with a plum role. He finally agreed to the casting. But *Country Girl* would indeed present Grace with a daunting challenge. The part of Georgie Elgin was totally unglamorous. It came complete with drab wardrobe and little makeup. It was a far cry from Hitchcock's shimmering presentation of her, in color, in *Rear Window*. In this black-and-white film, she would be portraying a plain, bitter young woman married to an alcoholic has-been, a former star (Crosby) attempting a Broadway comeback.

Crosby, for the first time in his long career, was undertaking an un-sympathetic role, but one with strong Oscar-winning possibilities. Nonetheless, he was very nervous about it. Only a few years earlier, polls had rated Academy Award–winner Crosby—he'd won 1945 Best Actor for playing a priest in *Going My Way*—as "the most admired man alive." He remained one of the most popular singers of all time. But Crosby's "Mr. Nice Guy" image, personifying the ultimate family man with wife and four sons, was tired. And belied the fact, according to Crosby son Gary and others, that Bing was a cold man. In public, "I would see Dad change into 'Bing Crosby,'" recalled Gary, but in private, "I was afraid of him."

Bill would be portraying the director of the play, a strong-willed man who falls in love with Georgie. Any similarities between Holden's real-life drinking problem and that of Crosby's character were not a topic of conversation, although Crosby was an expert on the subject. He warned his sons to stay away from alcohol, because "it killed your mother."

Director George Seaton was happy with his cast. He'd directed Crosby the previous year in a dramatic role, in *Little Boy Lost*. And he was happy to discover that Bill Holden was a screen actor "with great technical expertise" and was amazed by his knowledge of the medium. "His instincts were always on target, not only about his role but how it related to the others," said Seaton. He observed that the three stars "worked as a team" and didn't try to "shoot off in a different direction and give solo performances." Seaton also noted that both Bill and Bing "helped Grace."

The tedious, worrisome job of making a movie, with the actors sequestered most of the time from the "real" world, offered the usual spare time for mischief. Intimacy to alleviate the boredom was a foregone conclusion, and Grace and Bing began a discreet affair. Crosby asked Bill not to interfere, and Holden, at first, complied. Crosby, of Irish lineage—Harry Lillis "Bing" Crosby Jr.—was ready to get married again. His wife of twenty years, former actress Dixie Lee, had died only two years earlier. Bing considered Grace "a fiery Irish girl," suitable wife material. She turned down his proposal (three years later, at age fifty-four, Crosby married twenty-four-year-old actress Kathryn Grant).

As production progressed, what had been a romantic interlude for Bill and Grace during *Bridges at Toko-Ri* now, post-Crosby, became a serious relationship. Grace, like Audrey, fell in love with the irresistible Holden. The assistant director on the film, Mel Dellar, a friend of Bill's, later said: "Bill was absolutely crazy about her, and they had quite a fling." For Grace it was more than a fling, and she brought Bill home to meet her family. He wasn't prepared for the experience—the Kelly clan, ensconced at the family beach house in Ocean City, New Jersey, was a voluble, volatile group. It was hardly the ultracivilized encounter that transpired when Audrey had introduced Bill to her mother, the baroness. Jack Kelly, Grace's father, was a self-made multimillionaire, handsome as any movie star, with a temper to match. He was tough in every way (he'd had Ray Milland investigated) and was suspicious of Holden's intentions. It was apparent that he disliked him almost on sight, which was not an uncommon experience with the boyfriends Grace brought home.

Holden was not accustomed to anyone not liking him. Kelly, not in the least impressed by Holden's importance in the movie business, demanded to know what was going on between him and Grace. He looked Bill in the eye and said, in a sinister tone, "Bill, aren't you married?" Grace lied to her father, telling him they weren't having an affair. But her father confronted Bill. Holden told Kelly to go to hell and stormed out. Grace was in tears.

What followed was a replay of what had happened with Bill and Audrey—Bill and Grace simply continued their romance at her apartment on Sweetzer Avenue in West Hollywood. Bill took Grace to many of the out-of-the-way spots he had taken Audrey; they were careful not to be together at the studio, or in their dressing rooms. When word began getting around, the response was that Grace was always chaperoned, often by one of her sisters. But Grace wasn't as fortunate as Audrey. *Confidential* magazine broke the story, complete with photos of Holden's white Cadillac Eldorado convertible parked outside of Grace's apartment. In the corridors of power at MCA and Paramount, and at the Kelly family compound, there was anger, dismay, and concern.

In Audrey Hepburn's world, there must have been sighs of relief— perhaps dumping Bill and marrying Mel was the smartest thing she ever did. At the time, that seemed a reasonable assumption.

At least with Audrey and Bill the drama had remained behind the scenes. Now, Grace's father and champion athlete brother, John Jr. ("Kell"), charged into *Confidential*'s offices and roughed up some of the editors, which only made more news, and it certainly did not make the story go away. The damage was done. Grace as femme fatale wasn't what her agents, the studio, or her family had in mind.

Soon it was Grace's turn for dinner-at-Ardis's. The studio was utilizing the same strategy that had successfully diffused the Audrey-and-Bill romance. The difference, as far as Ardis was concerned, was that Bill's feelings for Grace were not those he'd had for Audrey. Obviously, she did not have to regard Grace with anything more than benign envy. Damage control, nonetheless, was on high alert. What about all the incriminating stories and gossip? Nonsense! Would the beautiful Mrs. Holden (an actress herself), ever welcome her husband's girlfriend into her home? Hardly.

Why had Holden's automobile been parked in front of Grace's apartment? Because, said Grace, he was simply giving her a lift to his home, where she would be having dinner with both Bill and Mrs. Holden. "That was my romance with Bill," she said, dismissing as absurd any other implications. For the most part, this approach worked. Hedda Hopper, however, pulled no punches: she said she thought Grace was a nymphomaniac. But Hedda, now seventy years old, was persuaded not to pursue this line of gossip.

Holden later confided to a close friend, actor Broderick Crawford, that he had discussed marriage with Grace, and she had told him that if he converted to Roman Catholicism, his marriage to Ardis wouldn't be valid in the eyes of the church and then she and Bill could be married in a religious ceremony. Although she thought she'd provided him with the perfect plan, it backfired: "I'd be damned if I'd let any church dictate what I could do with my life," said Bill.

So neither Audrey nor Grace was destined to achieve her heart's desire to become Mrs. William Holden. It was Bill, dapper in a black tuxedo, a broad smile on his face, who graciously presented the Best Actress Oscar to Grace for her performance in *The Country Girl*. By then their affair was over.

The win was a stunning surprise—Judy Garland, in *A Star Is Born*, had been expected to take the prize. Judy later complained, "I didn't appreciate Grace Kelly taking off her makeup and walking away with my Oscar." But Grace played the moment to the hilt. Beautiful and aristocratic in a blue satin, floor-length creation, wearing white opera gloves, an evening purse dangling from a chain on her wrist (this began a fashion trend), Grace modestly accepted the statuette from Bill's hands: "The thrill of this moment," she said emotionally to the audience, "prevents me from saying what I really feel."

Audrey had been nominated as Best Actress for *Sabrina*, but losing to Grace was not a shock. To Audrey, the shocking winner that year was Edith Head. Audrey had been under the impression that she had retained Head's goodwill, despite having worn Givenchy in *Sabrina*. But Edith felt betrayed, and on Oscar night she had her revenge: *Sabrina* won the award for best costume design, and Head accepted the award as her own, with no mention of Givenchy in her speech. Furthermore, his name did not appear in the credits of the film. Audrey vowed she'd make it up to her dear friend Hubert.

~•~

It was bound to happen. A year had passed, and now Audrey and Grace stood only a few feet apart in the wings, formally gowned, posture-perfect, both looking divinely beautiful, nervously waiting to go on.

It was live television and anything could go wrong. It was March 21, 1956, at the RKO Pantages Theatre in Hollywood, and the Oscar-cast was in progress.

Because Grace was the previous year's winner for *The Country Girl,* she would be presenting the Best Actor Oscar. Audrey was presenting Best Picture. Host Jerry Lewis's unmistakable voice, drawing laughter and applause from the audience, could be heard clearly backstage as he joked about the evening's anxious nominees. Hepburn and the rest of Hollywood, including Bill, had been taken aback by Grace's announcement, only months before, that she would be retiring—retiring!—from filmmaking, at the age of twenty-seven, to marry an actual prince, Rainier III of Monaco.

Knowledgeable as Audrey, her mother, and their family were about European royalty, she knew that Grace had not stumbled upon a real-life, *Roman Holiday*–type fairy tale come true, even though to the press and public it seemed that way. The facts were that Prince Rainier needed to produce a male heir if his family's rule was to continue. Otherwise, by treaty, Monaco would become a French protectorate.

"Along came Grace, beautiful, fiscally sound, and, best of all, fecund [fertile]," wrote Kelly family biographer Arthur Lewis. Monaco was not exactly Great Britain; it was a tiny oasis for billionaires, a tax haven and gambling mecca known, up to then, as Monte Carlo. The prince himself had quite a history. The latest woman he had been in love with was French actress Gisèle Pascal, who couldn't bear children and wanted to continue her career. She had ended their four-year royal relationship by having an affair with Gary Cooper.

Audrey was hardly jealous of Grace; she was welcome to her prince, and all that came with him. It was a "golden cage" she was stepping into. For Grace, who would always remember how Philadelphia's Main Line society had snubbed her father, a genuine royal title was the ultimate payback. Family was all-important to Grace. When she had recently been in New York, having completed her final film, *High Society,* she was literally besieged by the press. Every important reporter wanted an interview, and every moment of her days was accounted for. But she slipped away one afternoon for an important personal reason: she had promised her niece, a budding figure skater, that she would watch her practice at the Iceland rink, located in the Madison Square Garden building at Fiftieth Street and Eighth Avenue. When Grace arrived at the rink, it didn't take long for the other skaters to realize who had just appeared. Grace was alone, dressed simply in a sleeveless blouse, a full skirt, a silk scarf around her neck, with huge dark sunglasses shielding her eyes. She took a seat on the sidelines, removed her glasses, and quietly observed the skaters. She smiled at the ones who skated over and asked for autographs, as did the parents who were also watching from the sidelines. This was nothing new for Grace's niece—"Auntie Grace" always caused commotion when she appeared in public.

That Oscar night at the Pantages Theatre, Kelly, who would be leaving for Monaco in two weeks, was breathtaking in a creation by Helen Rose. Audrey was equally stunning in Givenchy, appearing more fragile, even thinner, than Grace. Audrey's hairdo was a version of her familiar gamine look, with a petite chignon in back. Grace's blonde hair was dressed Greek goddess–style, shimmering, sleek, and stunning. Both women were the epitome of classic elegance.

At first, they barely acknowledged each other, each perhaps feeling a tinge of self-consciousness. Then Audrey turned, smiled at Grace, and wished her the very best of luck on her upcoming marriage and told her she thought she had been *wonderful* in *The Country Girl.* Grace graciously returned the smile, and the compliments. "They were like two prized hounds at a dog show," said an MCA executive who was there. "I thought Grace looked like the princess she was about to become, and Audrey matched her in attitude and looks."

Their mutual inamorato, Bill Holden, would be making a presentation that evening, too, but not in person; away on location, he'd be on film. In the theater was another person Audrey and Grace had in common—they had both dumped Edith Head. Audrey had bypassed her for Givenchy; and now Grace, Edith's "favorite"—Edith had created many memorable costumes on-screen for Grace and had been instrumental in creating Grace's fashion image—bypassed Edith for MGM's Helen Rose, who would be designing Grace's wedding gown.

Years later, Head wryly observed that Helen Rose was a perfect choice on Grace's part—after all, wasn't she also the designer of the costumes for the *Ice Capades*?

But on that Oscar night in 1956, Edith deserved an award for concealing her true emotions regarding the otherworldly Grace and Audrey, both of whom, in 1959, would be named to the prestigious International Best Dressed List, joining the duchess of Windsor and a select bevy of society notables.

PART II

Together Again

Chapter

7

IT WAS 1962. THE PUBLIC'S TASTES WERE CHANGING, AND SO was the motion picture industry. Audrey, Bill, and a select few others would outlast the studio system that had created them. But the days when stars, producers, writers, and directors would be placed under long-term contract were over. And so was the protection that the studio system had offered. For better or worse, the industry's top-of-the-line creative personnel were on their own, working on a film-by-film basis.

Since the mid-1950s, Audrey's home base had been in Switzerland, where she and Mel intended to buy an estate, once they found the right one. She considered Switzerland the safest, most civilized country, where one could maintain complete privacy. The tax structure was more than friendly. The major cities of Europe were less than a couple of hours away. And, when out and about, people might recognize you but they never bothered you. Most important, Switzerland was a wonderful place to raise children, with first-rate educational facilities and the finest clinics and doctors.

Bill was becoming a citizen of the world and, for tax purposes, he too had established a Swiss residence. He bought his family a beautiful home in Saint-Prex, near Lausanne. He was perfectly happy making films abroad—"I don't feel Hollywood is the center of motion picture production any longer," he observed accurately. He was loudly criticized by the Screen Actors Guild, for encouraging "runaway production," and by members of Congress, who labeled him a millionaire tax evader. Robert F. Kennedy, newly appointed attorney general of the United States, singled out Holden as a wealthy man typical of those "perverting the tax laws." Kennedy's wife, Ethel, "was heard to call William Holden a traitor for choosing to live in Switzerland." The Kennedys might have had personal reasons, which would emerge many years later, for being so anti-Holden. It seems reasonable to believe, based on revelations by historian Edward Klein, and by presidential historian Arthur Schlesinger Jr., that their enmity sprang from the fact that Jacqueline Kennedy had had an affair with Bill, and others, in response to her husband's dalliances with, among many others, Marilyn Monroe.

Bill couldn't have cared less about what was said about him, by the Kennedys or anyone else—he was following Billy Wilder's advice and traveling extensively, promoting and publicizing his movies. Holding onto a sense of purpose was becoming harder and harder, but a very encouraging development had taken place. Before having taken up residence in Switzerland, at the end of 1958, Bill had traveled to Kenya with his pals Ray Ryan, an oil tycoon, and Swiss banker Carl Hirshmann. Kenya, and its animal population, captured Bill's heart. He welcomed it as the very antithesis of Hollywood and its inhabitants.

He related in a very basic way to wild animals. They were in tune with his own nature, they were nonjudgmental, noncompetitive, "and go right for your soul," as many animal lovers have experienced. Bill told feature writer Joe Hyams, "Originally I planned to be the great white hunter with a Nikon camera, but when I got to Africa I found the boys depended on the hunters for meat. Before I knew it I was out shooting meat for camp, rugs for my children, and zebra skins for Billy Wilder's office. I don't believe in shooting anything you can't eat, walk on, or hang up." One trophy he hung up was the head of a beautiful gazelle, which he'd dubbed "the Audrey Hepburn" of gazelles because of its delicate long neck. Even wildlife reminded him of Audrey.

Bill would soon realize that he couldn't, nor did he want to, shoot animals for any reason—he wanted to preserve their lives, to "save nature from mankind." In partnership with Ryan and Hirshmann, he bought the Mawinga Hotel in Kenya, which sat on one hundred acres, located on the slope of Mount Kenya at an altitude of 6,900 feet. The partners planned to develop it into the Mount Kenya Safari Club for the preservation of game.

～•～

Still married to Ardis, and committed to his responsibilities to their three children, Bill nonetheless continued to weave in and out of other relationships. And from what he had been hearing, Audrey's marriage wasn't in the greatest shape, either.

When Audrey's agent informed her that under the terms of her original contract she owed Paramount a picture—and they wanted to re-team her with Bill Holden, who also owed them a picture—how did she feel about it? Was she comfortable with it? In the nine years since they had worked together on *Sabrina*, as far as anyone knew, Audrey and Bill had rarely encountered each other. On those occasions in Los Angeles, all was cordial and polite. Her attitude had never been: "No matter what, I'll never work with Bill Holden again." She harbored no ill feelings toward him; he would always occupy a special place in her heart.

She had moved on with her life. When she had told Bill that becoming a mother was more important to her than anything else in the world, she'd been truthful. She was a mother at last, and it had been a very difficult, at times dangerous, pregnancy (an earlier pregnancy had resulted in a stillborn child). Her marriage had survived several crises but was functioning well enough, or so she told herself; she had heard rumblings regarding Mel and other women almost from the beginning, but considering the business they were in, that was to be expected. They were both sophisticated people. He was an effective watchdog; everyone wanted something from Audrey and her personality required the right person, other than herself, to say no. Mel was very efficient at doing this.

In the years since *Sabrina*, both Audrey and Bill's careers had flourished—Bill's in particular, commercially speaking. After the two films with Grace Kelly, Holden starred with Jennifer Jones in *Love Is a Many Splendored Thing*. Bill had envisioned a different leading lady. When he had read Han Suyin's autobiographical *A Many-Splendored Thing*, he suggested to Paramount that they buy it for him and Audrey. But the rights had already been sold to 20th Century-Fox.

In *Picnic*, another big hit, Bill co-starred with beautiful twenty-three-year-old actress Kim Novak, further cementing his stature as one of Hollywood's most desirable and romantic leading men. Bill had also made a number of television appearances in the1950s, and Lucille Ball asked him to appear, as himself, on *I Love Lucy*. Holden and Lucy had made a movie together, *Miss Grant Takes Richmond*, six years earlier, and he had enjoyed the experience. Rarely was he offered an opportunity to play for laughs. The "light" side of Bill—and there was a light side—would be very much on display in the episode she had in mind, which was titled "LA at Last!" The prospect of playing comedy before a live audience terrified him, but Lucy prevailed. The episode became an instant classic. In a key scene, for plot reasons, Lucy is wearing a fake nose. Holden, cigarette lighter in hand, "accidentally" sets her nose on fire, and it's a slow burn. Both Bill and Lucy's reactions and interaction, are priceless. The ratings went through the roof; everyone, press and public alike, was laughing and talking about it the next day.

There were other appearances on friends' TV shows: Bob Hope, Jack Benny, and cutting-edge newcomer Steve Allen among them. Bill would good-naturedly trade barbs and engage in playful, self-deprecating repartee. He came across as extremely likable on these occasions, reinforcing in the public mind that he was accessible, a truly *nice* guy, which he essentially was.

Bill was voted, by motion picture theater exhibitors, the number-one box-office male star of 1956. The following year, he enjoyed tremendous acclaim for *The Bridge on the River Kwai,* a worldwide blockbuster directed by David Lean. (Cary Grant had been first choice; he turned it down because of what was certain to be arduous location filming.) In *Kwai,* there was no leading lady to tempt Bill, and Ardis visited him often on location. The film turned out to be what many considered the finest war, or antiwar, movie made up to that time. It swept the Oscars and was a financial bonanza for Bill; his deal guaranteed him a percentage of the gross, resulting in a $50,000 annual income for the rest of his life for that film alone. He was one of the highest-paid actors in America, at the top of most popularity polls. That did not decrease his insecurities regarding his talent. Holden derived little satisfaction from wielding superstar clout and was not known to go off on any power trips, unless provoked. There was a conflict within him, though, because he never approved of acting as a profession for a man.

Bill sometimes had to laugh at the lengths to which an actor would go for this profession. Paying a visit to the set of Billy Wilder's *Some Like It Hot,* he posed, a wry smile on his face, with Tony Curtis in full drag as "Geraldine," pouting glossed lips and all, and Bill's expression was dead-on. He said he didn't think he'd have the guts to tackle a role like that, mostly because he would look like a woman no man in his right mind would ever take a second look at.

Bill also knew this profession of his was inherently not conducive to a happy home life. During production of *The Horse Soldiers*, co-starring Holden with John Wayne under the direction of John Ford, he was asked by feature writer Phyllis Battelle about the ongoing rumors concerning his marriage. Bill took the easy way out: he lied. "I have no intention of considering marriage with anyone else but my wife." He said they were fortunate enough to have a family and had been able to work out any "difference of opinion," pointing out that it was not easy to do when his profession frequently took him away from home.

∼•∽

After *Sabrina*, Audrey learned how it felt to be connected with projects that were far more problematic. Whereas Holden was the type of star who rarely got involved in production matters, the team of Audrey and Mel went to town on *War and Peace*, a multimillion-dollar spectacle based on the Tolstoy novel, produced by Dino De Laurentiis and directed by King Vidor.

PR executive David Hanna was in the thick of it, and he recalled: "No two stars found more ways to keep themselves occupied than Mel and Audrey. They had their fingers in every piece of the production," and that included the script, casting decisions, and costume design. "Nothing escaped their eagle eyes," said Hanna, "and their influence accounted, in no small part, for the gross miscasting of Henry Fonda." Hanna had been looking forward to meeting Audrey; he had met Ferrer years earlier, when Hanna was a newspaperman and film critic, and found him "a bright, charming, show-wise actor and director." The two men shared an interest: old-time vaudeville. "We would match memories on the names of old acts, songs, and who did what in the heyday of the two-a-day," recalled Hanna.

On meeting Audrey, Hanna was surprised: "She turned out to be taller than I had imagined from the screen and not nearly so frail as she looked, at least to judge by her Joe Louis–like handshake." Hanna observed at once Audrey's "readiness to accept Mel's guidance." And Audrey wasted no time in letting Hanna know what she expected from him. "With rare directness, Audrey took me right into her confidence, telling me point-blank that Mel was not her Svengali, that the double Broadway curtain calls [during *Ondine*] stemmed from her insistence because she felt Mel, as a better-known New York player, deserved them." Audrey also told Hanna that if he were asked about their marriage, he should reply that she was very happily married "and proposed staying that way for some time."

She meant those statements. Her feelings for Mel were genuine. They loved each other, but it was not a Catherine-and-Heathcliff, Scarlett-and-Rhett—or Audrey-and-Bill—type of relationship. It's a safe assumption that Ferrer was a more-than-satisfying lover. Before meeting Audrey, he had built up quite a reputation as being no slouch in the romance department. In photographs of Mel and Audrey together, at times he seemed to assume a father-figure persona. When, years later, the couple was photographed by the legendary Bert Stern, he noted there was a very father-daughter dynamic in play between husband and wife. He photographed them that way: Ferrer, bearded and standing, looking down at Audrey, who was seated and gazing up at him.

Despite the couple's best efforts, *War and Peace* was not destined to be a classic, although it was a commercial success. Mel and fifty-two-year-old Fonda were Audrey's two leading men. Vying for her character's love, the trio hardly set the screen on fire.

Audrey's first all-out musical—*Funny Face*—opened big in select markets, but it was not, as most people believed, an across-the-board blockbuster. It was another Cinderella role, and "Hepburn Sings! Hepburn Dances!" was the "hook." All the talents—except for Arthur Freed—that had produced the classic MGM musicals were associated with this Paramount film, including *Singin' in the Rain* and *Seven Brides for Seven Brothers* director Stanley Donen. Fred Astaire, at fifty-seven, was twenty-seven-year-old Audrey's leading man (Hepburn received top billing). The brilliant Kay Thompson was featured, and many felt she stole the show.

Audrey's singing and dancing in the film delighted her fans, and the photographs produced to publicize the numbers have since become iconic, even appearing in memorable Gap advertising campaigns for "skinny pants" decades later. In *Sabrina*, Audrey had sung one song, "La Vie en Rose," interpolated into a nonmusical film, and it worked perfectly. Performing all-out, full-fledged musical numbers was something else entirely. Audrey wasn't completely candid, years later, when she said that dancing with Astaire was "just as marvelous as people think it would be. Made me feel like a terrific dancer." According to Kay Thompson, Astaire felt differently, and Hepburn admitted to Thompson that working with Astaire had been "a strain." Audrey was indisputably dazzling in the film's fashion sequences, for which Richard Avedon was special visual consultant. "I will forever be devastated by the gift of Audrey Hepburn before my camera," said Avedon. For fashionistas, Hepburn in *Funny Face* was, and remains, a sensation, and even today young women connect to it.

Audrey and Mel ventured onto television, not for the first time, but this time they were paid a record $250,000 to star together in

Mayerling, the tragic love story of Crown Prince Rudolf of Austria and his mistress, the Baroness Maria Vetsera. It was far too ambitious a production for "live," studio-bound TV, and it was clumsily staged. Interestingly enough, there was little chemistry on-camera between Audrey and Mel. Reputations weren't wrecked, but the couple never acted together again. During production, they were happy living in director Anatole Litvak's beautiful and peaceful home, a three-level beachfront house with breathtaking views, located on the Pacific Coast Highway north of Santa Monica, California. There they indulged their passion for playing Ping-Pong.

Audrey was pleased that Mel was having a good year professionally; he starred with Tyrone Power, Ava Gardner, and Errol Flynn in Darryl Zanuck's production of Ernest Hemingway's *The Sun Also Rises*, which turned out to be a disappointment for all concerned. "It got loused up somewhere," noted Gardner.

People were surprised to learn that Mel, too, had a "light" side. He was a guest panelist on the top-rated TV game show *What's My Line?* A playful Mel smiled, sometimes laughed, and overall seemed to be having a good time along with panelists Arlene Francis, Dorothy Kilgallen, and Bennett Cerf, as they tried to guess contestants' occupations. The "mystery guest" that week was thirty-eight-year-old Lana Turner. The panelists, donning eye masks, had to guess who it was, asking questions while the mystery person, in an assumed voice, squeaked an answer. After Lana's identity was revealed and panelists' masks came off, Mel was delighted to see her, and it was mutual. They knew each other well from their MGM days. She referred to him affectionately as "our Mel," and they embraced warmly as she made her exit. Audrey was one of the few superstars who never made a "mystery guest" appearance on the show (Bill Holden did).

American audiences bypassed what should have been, at the very least, a succès d'estime for Audrey: *Love in the Afternoon,* which re-teamed her with *Sabrina* producer-director Billy Wilder. Audrey starred with another legend, Gary Cooper. Wilder's first choice, once again, had been Cary Grant. So far, Audrey had been leading lady to Bogart, Fonda, Astaire, and now Cooper, all of whom were old enough to be her father. The Cooper pairing was, at times, ludicrous. A nonmajor company, Allied Artists, distributed the film, which performed poorly in America. In Europe it did well, a tribute to Audrey's overseas appeal.

George Stevens wanted her for the title role in his film of *The Diary of Anne Frank.* She turned it down. It struck too close to home. The similarities between her and Anne Frank would bring back too many painful memories of her own wartime youth. Audrey would revisit the material decades later, in another venue. She also turned down the role of the Japanese bride, opposite Marlon Brando, in *Sayonara,* saying people would laugh at her attempting to be an "Oriental." "No one would believe me," she said. "I know what I can and can't do . . . I would be terrible." One wonders how she would have felt playing the Eurasian opposite Bill in *Love Is a Many Splendored Thing.*

She scored a major success, worldwide, with *The Nun's Story,* a production that was a grueling physical ordeal for everyone involved. This one was special, and its impact, personally and professionally, remained with Audrey for the rest of her life. Directed by Fred Zinnemann, Audrey's portrayal of a deeply conflicted young woman intent on becoming a nun but forced to confront her all-too-human beliefs and desires was magnificent. It was a tour de force that should have won her a second Oscar.

Many years later, Audrey's longtime companion, Robert Wolders, said that of all Audrey's films, he believed that *The Nun's Story* most accurately reflected the "real" Audrey—her introspective nature, the inner turmoil she suffered when faced with a not easily solved situation. Her son Sean said that her performance as "Sister Luke" was the one she was proudest of.

During production, Audrey had a very discreet affair with the film's screenwriter, forty-two-year-old Robert Anderson (Audrey was soon to turn thirty). Others in the company were aware of it; whether or not Mel knew is open to conjecture. He wasn't on site. The Ferrers were accustomed to long periods of separation, dictated by their careers. Looking the other way, perhaps, was, on occasion, the simplest way to maintain a show-business marriage. Ardis and Bill Holden could certainly have confirmed this.

Several years after *The Nun's Story*'s successful release, when it came time to cast the movie version of *My Fair Lady,* studio boss Jack Warner cited "what Audrey Hepburn did for exhibitors with *The Nun's Story*" as one of the major reasons he wanted her for what would be the most expensive musical made up to that time. Theater owners would pay enormous advances knowing that she would be the star of the picture.

Bill and the rest of the industry were stunned to learn that Audrey broke her back, literally, and suffered a miscarriage while making *The Unforgiven.* Burt Lancaster co-starred, and it was directed by the revered John Huston, whom Gregory Peck once described as "a bit of a snake-oil salesman." (Huston had directed Peck in *Moby Dick.*) "I would have killed that son-of-a-bitch Huston," Bill Holden told publicist Arthur Jacobs.

Filmed on location in Mexico, *The Unforgiven* was Audrey's first— and last—Western, a film both she, and Huston, rarely discussed later on. Audrey, in the role of what was then described as a half-breed, was offbeat casting, to say the least. Her role would involve horseback-riding sequences. Audrey was a novice, and afraid of horses; still, instead of using a stunt double, Huston, who liked to challenge his stars to perform stunts as a test of their integrity as artists, talked her into it. Audrey fell off her horse, broke her back, and lost her baby. It was a traumatic time, physically and mentally, and Mel nursed her through it. They were living in a home on Kimridge Road in Beverly Hills, and Mel has recalled, "The house looked like a hospital ward."

To divert her, and take her mind off the pain, Mel brought home a baby deer. It was originally named Pippin and nicknamed "Ip." She fell in love with the doe, who slept in the bathtub, and for a while "Ip" shared Audrey's affections with her adored Yorkshire terrier, Mr. Famous. Famous was her most precious possession. She loved him and he went with her everywhere. No matter what problems she faced, Mr. Famous was there to cheer her up. Even Mel had described him as "a renowned scene-stealer." He had appeared fleetingly in a fashion sequence in *Funny Face*.

"Ip" was going to be used in *Green Mansions*, a film to star Audrey with newcomer Anthony Perkins (like Audrey, another William Wyler discovery). The big news was that Mel was going to direct. It would be the first of many films he planned to direct starring his wife. A lot was riding on it. The property, which had been knocking around MGM for years, was based on William Henry Hudson's well-known novel, *Green Mansions: A Romance of the Tropical Forest*. The film turned out badly, and Mel would not direct Audrey in another. "Audrey, as Rima, the Bird Woman, lays an egg," quipped one critic. Mel's dream—of enjoying a Vivien Leigh-Laurence Olivier–type partnership with his wife—was over.

Audrey took a year off, and on July 17, 1960, Sean Hepburn Ferrer was born. Her return to the screen, in 1961, was spectacular in another signature role as memorable as the characters she played in *Roman Holiday* and *Sabrina*. *Breakfast at Tiffany's* cast an unlikely Audrey as Holly Golightly, a role author Truman Capote had wanted his friend Marilyn Monroe to play (both actresses were a decade too old for the character as conceived by Capote in his novella). Directed by Blake Edwards, from a script by George Axelrod, the dark story morphed into a romantic comedy drama, providing Audrey with a vibrant new image—she was no longer the sprite or a childlike Cinderella. She would be "a wild thing," a free spirit, sophistication incarnate. At times she would have an upswept hairdo, her brunette locks streaked with highlights; other times, pigtails. Her persona would take on the edge of a young woman who was, essentially, an escort—in less polite terms, a prostitute—on the prowl for a rich husband. Capote had conceived her as "a tough character, not an Audrey Hepburn type at all." Hepburn assumed a whole new attitude on-screen: "I don't want to own anything until I can find a place where me and things go together," Holly explains. "I'm not sure where that is, but I know what it's like. It's like Tiffany's. . . ."

Givenchy created her wardrobe, and their collaboration made fashion history. In the opening sequence—which, over the years, has acquired a life of its own—the image of Audrey was unforgettable: on a very early New York morning, a taxi drives up a deserted Fifth Avenue and stops at Tiffany's. Audrey emerges from the taxi. She is wearing oversized, dark sunglasses and a stunningly simple, sleeveless, black sheath floor-length evening dress. Around her neck is fastened a bold, perfectly scaled faux-pearl bib, a jewel-encrusted medallion at its center, her earrings perfectly scaled to match. An ornament is fastened into her dramatic upswept hairdo.

With a wisp of a filmy white scarf draped over one arm, she carries a paper bag containing coffee and a Danish. She opens the bag, takes out the coffee, sips it, nibbles on the Danish, and gazes into Tiffany's windows; walking slowly, she turns the corner, then heads down a deserted Fifty-seventh Street, disposing of the coffee and Danish in a rubbish can along the way.

Posed studio shots of Audrey in versions of this regalia became instant iconic images and, to the present day, best-selling posters. Her props were a footlong cigarette holder, which she knew how to use, and the cat that plays a major role in the story. The many hats and accessories she wore in the film have forever after left an immeasurable impact on the world of fashion. "My look is attainable," Audrey noted on more than one occasion. "It's so easy! Women can look like Audrey Hepburn by flipping out their hair, buying the large sunglasses, and the little sleeveless dresses."

During location filming, Audrey shopped at the Bonwit Teller department store on Fifth Avenue, which was next door to Tiffany's. "When she got onto the elevator," recalled native New Yorker Sharon Silverfarb, "everybody instantly knew who she was. She wasn't aloof, or pretending not to notice that everyone noticed her, she was friendly, acknowledged everyone with a nod of her head, and smiled. She looked gorgeous, very simply dressed—that in itself was dramatic. Anyone in that elevator who was not an Audrey Hepburn fan before she got in that elevator certainly was by the time she got off." It was typical—Audrey was always courteous to her fans, and she willingly signed autographs.

Bill Holden was in New York around this time. He attended a Broadway show, solo, and afterward dropped in at Sardi's for a drink. Hy Gardner, a veteran reporter (and Hedda Hopper's former assistant), went over to chat with him. Recalling the *Sabrina* days, and all the gossip regarding Audrey and Bill, he asked Bill if he intended to say hello to Audrey, whose photograph was in New York's newspapers virtually every other day, as *Breakfast at Tiffany's* was being filmed all over Manhattan. "It's always a pleasure saying hello to Audrey," he responded, smiling, not at all upset by the question and its implications; in fact, he seemed genuinely pleased that Gardner had asked the question.

~·~

Tiffany's was a block away from Universal's offices, which were at 445 Park Avenue. One morning, when *Breakfast at Tiffany's* was filming, publicity executive Jerry Evans strolled over to the site to say hello to his counterpart from Paramount. During a break he was introduced to Audrey, who would soon be making a film for Universal, and Evans was charmed by her good manners. "So many stars I'd met and worked with were 'tough characters' off-camera. Hepburn looked you in the eye, had a strong handshake, a beautiful smile, and my feeling was that she wouldn't be a problem at all to work with."

The role of Holly Golightly, which she initially balked at playing, struck a chord. There were rumors that she was having an affair with her handsome, blond co-star, George Peppard. And there were rumors that they couldn't stand each other. Whatever the truth offscreen, on-screen their chemistry was authentic. The happy ending tacked onto the film resulted in a movie with wide appeal, although Truman Capote was never happy with it.

Audrey was surprised and delighted that her voyage into non-Cinderella territory had worked so well. As she had in *Sabrina*, she sang one song in the film—a plaintive new ballad, *Moon River*, by Johnny Mercer and Henry Mancini. The producers wanted to cut it, but Audrey fought to retain it. The song went on to win the Oscar, became a standard, and Audrey was nominated for an Oscar as Best Actress for the fourth time.

The movie won Audrey many new fans while delighting her loyal following. If anyone had told her and the filmmakers that they had made a film of cultural and historical significance, they would have dismissed the statement as ridiculous. However, decades later, *Breakfast at Tiffany's* would be added to the National Film Registry. Over the years there would be attempts to turn the material into a Broadway musical, which ran less than a week, then into a straight play without much better results. In critics' estimations, each actress attempting to portray Holly fell far short of the original.

The Children's Hour was the other film Audrey made the year she did *Tiffany's*. It had reunited her with director William Wyler, and co-starred Shirley MacLaine and James Garner, but the heavy drama failed to find an audience.

It was around this time that Audrey suffered an agonizing loss—her beloved Yorkie, Mr. Famous, dashed out into traffic near her California home. He was run over and killed.

Chapter

8

A PICTURE REUNITING AUDREY AND BILL COULDN'T POSSI-
bly bomb.

Considering the two stars' stature, Paramount was willing to rene-
gotiate payment terms on their old contracts. Audrey had been paid
less than $8,000 total for *Roman Holiday*. Her salary now, to complete
her commitment to Paramount, would be over $12,000 per week, with
plenty of perks, financial and otherwise, such as limousine and driver.
If the film went over schedule, there would be increased weekly com-
pensation. Holden would have a similar arrangement. Since both had
reputations as total professionals, it was unlikely the film would run
over schedule. If anything, it would be completed early. Neither Audrey
nor Bill would have a percentage of the gross or profits.

This time, Holden would receive top billing. Holden and Hepburn—a
potential box-office gold mine, and surely a jewel in each of their careers. The chosen vehicle was a romantic comedy, based on a French
film, *Holiday for Henrietta*, by Julien Duvivier and Henri Jeanson. The
new script was a spoof of Hollywood in which Holden would portray
a screenwriter, Audrey his Givenchy-clad secretary, and they would live
out his fantasy scenarios. Realism was not the order of the day; glamour
and fun, with an edge, were the keynotes.

Paris When It Sizzles would be filmed in widescreen and color. The
writer was George Axelrod, who had written the script for *Breakfast at*

Tiffany's. The producer-director, Richard Quine, was hardly a Wyler, Wilder, Zinnemann, King Vidor, or David Lean. A former actor, he had directed Kim Novak (whom he almost married) in several films, and he had recently directed Bill in the hit *The World of Suzie Wong.* Audrey had doubts; she met with Quine, who flew to Switzerland to convince her. She liked him, was candid in discussing her doubts and fears, and then gave her okay.

The film would be made in Paris, one of Audrey's favorite cities, and one of the reasons she agreed to do the picture. She had many Parisian friends and loved the shops, restaurants, and everything else Paris had to offer. There would be location work all over the city. Givenchy would be close by to ensure perfection of her wardrobe, and because of the many fantasy sequences in the script, she would have a series of fabulous, in some cases outrageous, outfits, plus many wigs and accessories to play around with. Givenchy even designed a cover for the birdcage Audrey's character carries around in several of the scenes.

Audrey was looking forward to working with Bill again, this time for pure fun. He was a wonderful actor. Now she didn't need a lover or a protector and there would be no dressing-room rendezvous, no private ballet performances for Bill, no dining and dancing by candlelight in out-of-the-way spots—and no dinner with Ardis. Aware that there would be rumors linking them romantically, Audrey wasn't bothered.

To her, this time it would be a strictly professional collaboration that both she and Bill could be proud of and enjoy. Two artists at the peak of their abilities, seasoned by life and love.

"I remember the day I arrived at Orly Airport for *Paris When It Sizzles*," Bill recalled. "I could hear my footsteps echoing against the walls of the transit corridor, just like a condemned man walking the last mile. I realized that I had to face Audrey and I had to deal with my drinking. And I didn't think I could handle either situation." Over the years, he had tried to put Audrey out of his mind. He couldn't always manage that. And now he had become romantically involved with one of her best friends.

∽•⌣

She had been one of Givenchy's top models in the 1950s; that's how she and Audrey met, before either of them knew Bill. Germaine Hélène Irène Lefebvre, born in Saint-Raphaël, Var, France, was a year older than Hepburn, and a beauty along the same lines: tall, brunette, superb bone structure, mannequin-like figure, a velvety speaking voice. Unlike Audrey, she did not project vibrant innocence; her "vibe" was that of a femme fatale, at least on the surface. She was the opposite of Audrey when it came to her volatile relationship with her parents; she bristled at her strict Catholic upbringing, and she was headstrong and rebellious. Her beauty camouflaged other facets of her personality. She was also emotionally needy and sensitive, and suffered bouts of depression, a malady Audrey was not unfamiliar with. "Oh, I feel blue sometimes," Audrey later admitted, "but I'm never so depressed that I have to rush to a doctor."

As with Audrey, from the beginning Germaine wanted to make something of herself and could not wait to be out on her own. Desperately unhappy at home, she ran away to Paris and at eighteen years old, married French filmmaker Pierre Trabaud. They were divorced within a year.

Germaine hated her name, changing it to the evocative "Capucine" (pronounced Cap-u-seen), a name derived from an exotic South American plant. Friends called her "Cap," for short. Her route to the big time was more conventional than Audrey's: while modeling in New York City in the 1950s, she had been spotted by scouts for mega-agent/producer Charles K. Feldman, who subsequently fell in love with her. She was a young woman who knew when it was important to appear as remote as possible, when to be flirtatious and provocative, and when to release all inhibitions. She was adept at dealing with difficult, ambitious, high-powered men.

She appeared in several European films, but it was Feldman who eventually brought her to Hollywood. He paid for her acting lessons and secured important contracts for her. She won acclaim for *Song Without End,* and was John Wayne's leading lady in *North to Alaska. Walk on the Wild Side,* produced by Feldman, brought her worldwide attention. She played a call girl, whose madam—none other than Barbara Stanwyck—falls in love with her.

Capucine wanted to marry Feldman, but there was an obstacle: there was already a Mrs. Feldman, and social powerhouse Jean Howard Feldman was intractable in her desire to maintain the status quo. Capucine met Bill, another of Feldman's clients, when she was cast as Bill's leading lady in *The Lion,* a film produced by Feldman that was set in Africa.

Feldman was not upset when Bill and Capucine became lovers; in fact, he had given his approval, although Bill still felt guilty about it. When Audrey first learned about her friend's interest in Bill, and vice versa, it's certain that Audrey clued her in on what to expect. Cap was never jealous of Audrey; she was launched on a successful career of her own. She valued Audrey as someone she could confide in. They enjoyed the usual girl talk about skin care—both had a tendency to very dry skin, not an asset as far as the camera was concerned, and were patients of the finest Swiss dermatologists. Both women tended to lose too much weight too easily. And Cap, too, had been subjected to the Ardis experience.

Bill's marriage was indeed unusual, even in the topsy-turvy world of show business, where many led multilayered lives. Bill stayed married to Ardis because their state-of-the-union still suited them both. When together, it often seemed they were role-playing à la George and Martha in *Who's Afraid of Virginia Woolf?* Certainly there was tension aplenty when Mrs. Holden came to visit her husband on *The Lion*'s African location.

～•～

No one expected Bill to be in such bad shape on arrival in France for *Paris When It Sizzles*. There was no way of predicting when a period of sobriety would suddenly end; Bill's latest was obviously over. He'd slipped back into the bottle. There was a press conference to kick off the start of production, and Bill looked good in what had to have been a $2,000 dark suit. Audrey was beautiful in an ensemble by Givenchy. But things soon went downhill.

There was a pattern: first Bill drank to get his nerves under control, and when that didn't work, he drank some more. Director Richard Quine, who was familiar with Bill's "warm-up-the-ice-cubes" routine after a hard day's work, was shocked to find him in such a state. "Bill was like a punch-drunk fighter, walking on his heels, leaning slightly, talking punchy. He didn't know he was drunk."

Audrey was at a loss. Her former prince charming was a total mess; his playful vigor sadly diminished. Capucine had told her he had been fine, more or less, on the picture they had just done together; but she hadn't known him in the *Sabrina* days. Audrey was greatly distressed to see Bill's striking good looks in such disrepair. The smile still lit up a room, but when his face was in repose the wear and tear was evident. Only forty-four, he seemed gaunt, not fit, and his once-perfect nose had grown slightly bulbous from the excessive drinking. The death at age fifty, three years earlier, of his contemporary Errol Flynn, a bloated victim of alcohol and drug abuse, apparently struck no cautionary note.

There were days when Bill was sick-drunk, unable to work, and the production had to close down. Director Quine was not at all sympathetic (he was having his own troubles in his relationship with Kim Novak). At one point, Quine literally throttled the screen's former Golden Boy, whose attitude seemed to be that he could stop drinking any time he wanted to, only he didn't want to. Audrey's attitude was one of quiet understanding and compassion. So much had changed. She had become a mother and was now in her thirties. It was heart-wrenching for her to observe Bill becoming unglued. Bill misinterpreted her attitude of genuine concern as the return of her old feelings for him. When he realized that wasn't the case—that the only signals she was sending out were those of sympathy, which he interpreted as pity—he bitterly went on a binge. Trying to push aside the past took an almost herculean effort—the torch could still be blinding. The ever-protective Audrey often put herself in the line of fire to deflect attention from Bill's bad behavior. "All I did was mother him a little," she later said. "Anyway, I'm glad that Capucine is now getting all the publicity."

The decision was made for Bill to enter a rehab clinic, the Clinique du Chateau de Garches. So that filming could continue without him, a frantic Axelrod and Quine came up with a temporary solution: They brought in stars to do "cameo" appearances. They wouldn't receive billing, but with any luck, audiences would revel in wondering who would appear on-screen next, à la Mike Todd's *Around the World in 80 Days*. A call for help went out to Tony Curtis for the hastily written role of a producer. Curtis, too, had issues with drinking, but under the circumstances was on his best behavior. "I understood Bill's torment," he said. "You have to want to climb out of that hole. No one can do it for you."

Axelrod wrote brief scenes—no dialogue—for Mel Ferrer (wearing a Dr. Jekyll–Mr. Hyde mask at a costume party). Ferrer was around from time to time during production, and his presence made Bill nervous, his "Smiling Jim" grin emerging frequently . For Marlene Dietrich, who at sixty-two looked ageless and beautiful, there was a scene of her exiting a limousine, dressed in white. Dietrich and Audrey were friends. They had first met when she came to the *Sabrina* set eight years ago. "Too bad she can't play Holden's role," quipped studio chief Martin Rackin, on seeing the rushes of Dietrich's brief scene back in Hollywood.

That remark notwithstanding, Holden and Rackin were close friends. They had done a picture together, *The Horse Soldiers,* and years later, Rackin and his wife, Helen, would drive Bill to clinics when he needed treatment. So Bill was confident that at least he had strong support in the front office on this film. Rackin remembered Audrey as "nobody's fool, and she was never nasty or rude, or a pain in the ass. . . . Bill was a wonderful guy, with a terrible problem. I always tried to help."

Holden returned to work, looking and sounding much improved. In the meantime, other problems had emerged. Audrey was no longer an innocent regarding how she was photographed. The thirty-three-year-old was more aware than ever of how she looked on-screen, and, over the past five years, had undertaken subtle but extensive dental work to correct what she saw as flaws in her smile. Years later, she said that she thought plastic surgery was a wonderful thing, but one must do it in very small doses, over time, with the very best doctors, so nobody would be able to tell. (Bill, years later, would follow this advice when getting an eye lift.)

Franz Planer, who had been director of photography on *Roman Holiday*, *The Nun's Story*, *The Unforgiven*, *Breakfast at Tiffany's*, and *The Children's Hour*, had been Audrey's choice for *Paris*. "Uncle Franz" had played almost as important a role in Audrey's career as any director. He was ill and unable to accept this assignment.

Audrey agreed to Claude Renoir as cameraman. But on seeing the first rushes, she immediately regretted the choice and wasted no time in voicing that she wanted him replaced. Renoir was a legendary name in France and they were filming in Paris. For Audrey to have him replaced would be a scandal. The French unions would intercede, might even go on strike. There was no question, however: he had to go. Audrey was relieved that Charles Lang, the man who had photographed *Sabrina*, was available. Yes, he was slow and meticulous, but keeping Audrey looking her best and feeling happy was vital. The switch was accomplished over a weekend.

Noel Coward worked on the film for three days. Audrey sent him flowers, singing his praises, and so did Bill. Noel played a Hungarian film producer at a decadent costume party. He was dressed as Nero, complete with toga and bold gold jewelry. Noel wrote in his diary: "Bill Holden, off the bottle and looking fifteen years younger, absolutely charming to work with . . . Audrey and Bill are enchanting. So is Tony Curtis." Coward also noted that, on set, he and Bill exchanged confidences, "and bottles of eau-de-cologne during the interminable waits." Coward had an interesting observation after he'd been a houseguest of Audrey and Mel's. The couple had come outside to say good-bye, as he was about to get into his car. Of their good-byes-and-wonderful-to-see-you's, Coward later said: "The Lunts did it better."

Bill and Audrey's love scenes together in *Paris When It Sizzles* still had a spark, a tender intimacy that could not have failed to register with both of them. Being in such close, almost cruel proximity must have released the über-romantic in Bill. The look in her eyes, her voice. Bill had a way of performing romantic scenes before the camera that didn't intimidate or taunt his partner; if anything, she was more relaxed and able to express her own intimate feelings. And Audrey had learned how to playfully wring the most out of romantic dialogue. Bill was encouraged, and he was also naïve enough to believe that Audrey couldn't kiss him like that on-camera and not mean it.

One night, he impulsively climbed a tree by a wall leading up to her dressing-room window. He didn't do it quietly, and as she leaned out the window to find out where the noise was coming from, Holden leaned over to kiss her. "Bill, stop that!" she exclaimed. He fell out of the tree and landed on a parked car below.

His drinking started up again, and soon he was back in rehab for another "quick dry-out." The time was utilized filming other bits and pieces, including Audrey's close-ups, which were beautiful. Her makeup, too, had been masterfully refined over the years, and she was timelessly chic. Around this time, she was elected, for the third time, to the Fashion Hall of Fame.

The unit photographer on the film, Bob Willoughby, was a longtime friend of Bill and Audrey. He had been at Paramount in the *Sabrina* days. "I could see he was lonely, and needed someone to talk to," recalled Willoughby. "Everyone was in love with Audrey, but no one more than Bill."

Bill had bought a red Ferrari to cheer himself up. One day, driving drunk, he crashed the car into a wall. When he returned to the studio, he was on crutches and had one arm in a splint. Mrs. Holden was summoned to Paris to see if she could do anything to help her husband pull himself together. At forty-six, Ardis still looked good. She berated Bill and made no attempt to disguise her anger and contempt. There were shouting matches. Her appearance on the scene inspired Bill to even more outrageous behavior.

Audrey's marriage was not in stellar shape, either. Mel was very strict with her, like a father, and he had a temper. His acting career was alive, but hardly flourishing. Most recently, he had filmed a cameo for Darryl Zanuck's *The Longest Day*. He disliked acting, for reasons not unlike Bill Holden's: Ferrer labeled the profession "a self-conscious business" and said he was "a screaming schizoid," an introvert pretending to be an extrovert. "I curl up inside and freeze when I have to act. I much prefer sitting on the sidelines and trying to get the best out of other people." Unfortunately, his services as director were not in great demand, either. It was not the best of situations for a show-business marriage.

Audrey responded to his superior attitude by not making an issue of it. After all, he was Sean's father—and Bill Holden, on seeing Sean, became gloomy and despondent over the fact that he hadn't been able to have children with Audrey.

The troubled production finished shooting in October 1962, with Audrey eager to escape. Charlie Feldman and Marty Rackin were deeply concerned about Bill. He was grateful when Capucine, sent by Feldman, arrived on the scene to take care of him and help him through his next, difficult rehab at Chateau de Garches. He was thankful for her efforts, and took to referring to Cap as his Florence Nightingale.

Audrey told her agent that it had been a mistake to re-team her with Bill, and to try not to let it happen again. But perhaps the effort would prove to have been worth it. One could never tell how a picture, assembled start-to-finish, would play.

Chapter

9

"I T STINKS."

The words were clearly audible in the plush private screening room of Paramount's New York offices. Executives had just seen a rough assemblage of *Paris When It Sizzles*. Four months in production, overruns in cost because of Holden's absences (insurance covered most of it), and this was the result?

A saving grace: The great Nelson Riddle was going to compose the score, and there was a good chance Riddle's friend Frank Sinatra would sing the title song. But as far as the company's sales department was concerned, the film, in its current state, was unreleasable. It was shelved until they could figure out how to salvage it, or to market it so that it stood a chance of making some of its money back. The selling point was indisputable: Holden and Hepburn. It remained to be seen what the advertising/publicity/promotion boys would come up with to take full advantage of it.

This was not an unheard-of development in the movie industry. MGM was currently dealing with a similar situation regarding *Lady L*, a movie starring Paul Newman and Sophia Loren, megastars at the very height of their popularity. Despite the stars, and director Peter Ustinov's efforts (and that of other directors, including George Cukor, before him), it too simply didn't work and was being held for release.

There was always the remote chance they were wrong, and *Paris* would find an audience. Time would tell.

Bill's next film would be crucial in maintaining his reputation as an employable star; the industry knew about his behavior on *Paris*—could he be trusted to stay sober? *The Seventh Dawn* was an adventure drama, with Bill fighting Communist terrorists, to be filmed on location in Malaysia, far from the prying eyes of mainstream journalists. Capucine seemed the unlikeliest of choices to portray the leading lady, a Eurasian, although Cap, unlike Audrey, had no objections to playing an "Oriental." Co-producer Karl Tunberg, who also wrote the screenplay, voiced his objections—she was all wrong for the part. Surprisingly, Holden agreed. But Charlie Feldman was co-producing the film, and it was no surprise that Capucine was cast.

It was a tough location shoot, and director Lewis Gilbert had his hands full. The heat was almost unbearable. Makeup and hairdressing personnel had to contend with daily crises: keeping the actors looking camera-ready was a daunting task, when profuse perspiration virtually melted away the makeup. It was not a problem for Bill, who wore little or no makeup. But for Capucine, it was a nightmare. Her skin problems flared up; her makeup had to be reapplied several times during a shooting day, with her "Eurasian" eye makeup requiring frequent repairs. She looked far from her best and was hardly being *presented* in her role, as her friend Audrey had been presented in virtually all of her films to date.

Cap voiced plenty of complaints, but despite the adverse conditions, her love affair with Bill blossomed. Holden, drinking again, voiced no objections to their relationship becoming public. Nancy and Ronald Reagan, on a trip to the Far East, encountered their buddy Bill, and Nancy saw immediately that it was more than a temporary attraction between Holden and Capucine. She wrote her friend Ardis, alerting her to what was going on.

When *Seventh Dawn* wrapped, Bill fell seriously ill, a result of his drinking, which was wreaking havoc on his liver and other organs. He was flown to a hospital in Lausanne, where Capucine resided, and the actress visited him daily. Events took a potential quantum leap in drama when Ardis, living in the beautiful Holden home nearby in Saint-Prex, arrived in Lausanne. Once again, as though in a scenario from an old Hollywood tearjerker, wife and mistress found themselves face-to-face. Bill's condition worsened, and he was barely conscious most of the time, struggling to survive. By sheer coincidence, it was Capucine who was in the hospital room at those times he regained consciousness, and as far as Bill was concerned, she *was* his Florence Nightingale.

Bill's recuperative powers were amazing. He was finally pronounced out of danger and checked out of the hospital. He then informed Ardis that their marriage was over, and they legally separated not long afterward. He moved into an apartment in Lausanne, and a divorce seemed likely.

~•~

Audrey had finally landed Cary Grant as a leading man. He was almost sixty, and there would be no Bill Holden–like, sensual love scenes between the two stars. "There was no kissing," Audrey later recalled. "I don't think anyone noticed." The script for *Charade*, at Grant's insistence, had Audrey's character pursuing him; that prevented Grant's character from seeming like an older man lusting after a young woman. That would violate the legend of Cary Grant.

At first, she was intimidated by him. When they initially met over dinner, her nerves got the best of her. She accidentally knocked over a bottle of red wine onto his white suit. She was mortified. Cary didn't miss a beat; he simply removed his jacket, placed it on the back of his chair, asked Audrey to please not give it a second thought, and dinner proceeded without any further surprises.

Charade was a Hitchcock-like suspense thriller, to be filmed in Paris, and Audrey was delighted to play an aggressive (albeit gently aggressive) woman, a welcome first for her. The script, by Peter Stone, was excellent, and the supporting cast was stellar: Walter Matthau, James Coburn, and George Kennedy. Stanley Donen, with whom Audrey had enjoyed working on *Funny Face,* helmed the production. Audrey and Grant worked smoothly together. It was a huge contrast to working with Bill. Everything concerned Cary—camera placement, lighting, the works—as it should have because his company was co-producing the film with Donen and Universal. Audrey's relationship with Grant wasn't too different from the one he'd had with recent co-star Doris Day, who found him "a completely private person, totally reserved, and there is no way into him." It was not a case of him not being friendly or polite—"He certainly was," noted Doris. "But distant. Very distant."

When a rough cut of *Charade* was privately screened for Universal's New York publicity department, Fortunat Baronat, the company's New York–based foreign sales executive, proclaimed, in his thick accent: "It needs work!" Audrey and Mel subsequently stopped by to meet with Baronat to discuss upcoming overseas openings of the film. When word got around that Audrey was on the premises, the fourth-floor reception area suddenly became very lively as company personnel found reasons to hang around, hoping for a glimpse of the star. When she and Mel finally emerged from their meeting, Audrey smiled at the polite commotion she was causing. Requests for autographs were graciously granted. The couple glanced at their watches as they waited impatiently for the elevator. "We loved you in *Breakfast at Tiffany's*," said a young secretary. Mel answered: "Wait until you see *Charade!*"

There were meetings with other New York–based executives. Jerry Evans found the Ferrers very knowledgeable about the press, and very particular and specific about which publicity Audrey would and would not do. All requests had to be filtered through her personal PR man, the estimable Henry Rogers, founder of the Rogers and Cowan agency.

There was substantial editing before the film was considered ready for release. Henry Mancini's score, complete with title theme (lyrics by Johnny Mercer) that became a hit, pulled everything together nicely. From the beginning, there had been concern about the title—would American audiences know what it meant? (The British pronounced it "Shah-rahd.") The title remained.

For the first time in his career, in some scenes, Grant seemed overweight (a buttoned suit jacket could not conceal a tummy), with streaks of gray in his hair. In most scenes, though, he was trim as ever, no gray. His energy level was where it had to be, but he was contemplating retirement. He didn't intend to be a star playing roles he was too old for. He did retire within four years, and *Charade* was his last romantic leading-man role.

Like Grant, Audrey had no intention of going past that inevitable point when there would be a paucity of suitable roles for actors of a certain age. Even Audrey Hepburn wasn't immune from that reality, and she intended to bow out at the proper time. "I can't play the type of girls I portrayed early in my career after a certain point," she later said. "It wouldn't work. It would be fake."

For the time being, in *Charade* Audrey looked at all times youthful and beautiful. *Sabrina* cameraman Charles Lang, who had been working his magic since Cary Grant was a young leading man, did a masterful job.

Although there were no personal sparks between Hepburn and Grant off-camera, there was competition, publicity-wise. Both had photo approval, which they exercised assiduously. Audrey was a "pro" by now. She had come a long way since *Roman Holiday* and *Sabrina*. Grant was ultracareful to protect his own turf, involving himself personally when necessary. "It was all very civilized," recalled David Golding, Universal's overseas representative. "But it was real."

Audrey's impeccable wardrobe for the film was designed, of course, by Givenchy. Over the years, the designer's identification with the star's look had elevated him to a unique position in the fashion world; a photograph of Audrey was the sole signature required for L'Interdit (translation: "Forbidden"), a best-selling fragrance he created in her honor. Henry Rogers learned the hard way that Audrey would not tolerate criticism of Givenchy. Rogers expressed dismay that the designer had not provided her with complimentary L'Interdit—any promotion man in the business knew that she should have received cases of it. Nor, incredibly, was Audrey being paid for use of her photograph in advertising the product when her endorsement would have been worth a fortune. When Rogers voiced these concerns, Audrey promptly fired him. He subsequently told columnist Earl Wilson, off the record, that Audrey was "one of those Steel Butterflies, that's for sure."

But to be critical of Givenchy was to be critical of Audrey, their friendship, and all they both fervently believed in. For Audrey and Hubert, fashion was a religion, just as the theater was to Stanislavsky. Joan Juliet Buck, a novelist and former Paris *Vogue* editor, has explained: "Clothes are personal magic . . . [they provide] the same feeling that ingénues sing about on balconies in Broadway musicals; [they are] the concentrated essence of one woman's happiest times."

Mel was highly critical of the designer, for the same reasons Rogers had been—and he was furious that Audrey was billed full-price for clothes Givenchy created for her personal wardrobe. This was almost inconceivable, and Mel was vocal about it.

But Audrey was hardly about to fire Mel.

～•～

There is no record of Bill Holden's reaction when Audrey's fellow demi-goddess, Grace Kelly, after six highly publicized years as princess of Monaco, announced that she wanted to return to the screen. She was, in fact, desperate to resume her career. Disillusionment had set in, and Hepburn wondered how Grace could have stood it for so long inside that golden cage. She might have been a happier woman if she had married Bill Holden, sniped certain insiders. Grace had done her duty. She had provided the prince with heirs and had been the "perfect wife," although he was hardly the perfect husband. She explained to one of her close friends, "You've got to make compromises to make a relationship work." Grace was weary of compromising; rumors circulated that she was drinking and was considering a divorce.

Alfred Hitchcock had the perfect property—*Marnie*—and the perfect leading man, Sean Connery, fresh from his success as James Bond. Hitch flew to Monaco to discuss the project with the princess, whom he still called "Gracie," and was surprised at how tired and unhappy she looked.

"Connery will be a welcome respite from Prince Rainier," declared the British tabloids sarcastically. Universal was ecstatic, and the sales department was salivating at the prospect. The whopping financial terms they would be able to demand from exhibitors for Grace Kelly's comeback picture, especially in tandem with Hitchcock and Connery, would set new records and ensure overwhelming publicity.

Kelly's former agents, MCA, had bought Universal Pictures, and Lew Wasserman was running the show (he would soon be running the entire industry). All of her conditions would be met, including an astronomical $1 million for her services, which she planned to distribute to charities. Wasserman privately told associates he thought Grace's return wouldn't happen, but he negotiated in good faith. The excitement was short-lived. Prince Rainier said no, and Monaco's subjects didn't approve, either—it would be undignified and unbecoming for their princess to be engaging in "commercial" work, playing love scenes with a man not her husband. The script itself presented a monumental problem: the character, Marnie, was a liar and a kleptomaniac. Furthermore, Grace was privately informed that if she went ahead with the film, and with her plans to seek a divorce, she would never see her children again.

Her love, concern, and commitment to her two children was, like Audrey's for her son Sean, inviolable—Princess Caroline was then six, Prince Albert five, Stéphanie hadn't been born yet. Five decades later, at age fifty-six, Albert would recall that his mother "would have loved to have played the role in *Marnie*" but had made the more important choice: "She knew her duties and her commitment to her family were more important." He claimed, as any loving son would, that his father had left the choice completely up to her.

To date it remains the most spectacular screen comeback that never happened. At least Audrey still had the luxury of her career; she was soon to begin filming what many considered the plum role of the decade.

Paris When It Sizzles still sat on the shelf as Audrey started the nerve-racking, stress-filled task of preparing for, and filming, *My Fair Lady*. Whenever the subject of *Paris,* and reuniting with Bill on-screen, came up in interviews, Audrey always finessed her response so that it seemed the most natural thing in the world for the studio to delay its release; they were simply taking the time necessary to ensure that all was perfect. When Bill was asked if working with Audrey again had been all that he hoped it would be, his answer was that she was still the loveliest woman in the world, and that he could not have asked for a more enjoyable experience.

The industry's love affair with Audrey, however, ran into a stumbling block. She could not have anticipated the level of resentment rolling her way since she had accepted the *Fair Lady* role that "belonged" to Julie Andrews. She would pay the price later. Meanwhile, Jack Warner had paid a record price for her. With special clauses in her contract, and bonuses, she stood to gross comfortably over $1 million for the film, a feat accomplished by only one actress to that point—Elizabeth Taylor, for *Cleopatra*. Frings drove a killer bargain. Reports stated that Audrey would also receive a percentage of the gross (or profits, depending on which account proved accurate).

Audrey had *Charade* awaiting release; with the *Fair Lady* deal a fait accompli, if *Paris When It Sizzles* bombed, it would be little more than a blip in her career. For Bill, however, if *Paris* flopped, he would be in trouble. His last two films, *Satan Never Sleeps* and *The Counterfeit Traitor,* had been problematic. *Satan* was an outright flop, whereas *Traitor,* reuniting him with *Country Girl* director George Seaton, was first-rate, garnering sterling reviews. But though the film did well at the box office, it wasn't the kind of hit that generated excitement in the industry. For Holden, however, on a personal level, making the movie had enabled him to enjoy a closer relationship with his sons. Sixteen-year-old "West" (Peter) was an assistant to the still cameraman, and fourteen-year-old Scott worked in the men's wardrobe department.

Bill had made a gigantic career mistake in turning down *The Guns of Navarone* in 1960. The producers wouldn't meet his asking price: $750,000 and 10 percent of the gross. Gregory Peck was his replacement, and Peck's salary, plus that of co-stars David Niven and Anthony Quinn combined, did not add up to Holden's proposed salary. The picture was a megahit and would easily have maintained Holden's superstar status at an important juncture in his career.

In May 1963, Audrey attended a private birthday party for President John F. Kennedy. When he was Senator Kennedy, a decade earlier, he had said that *Roman Holiday* was his favorite picture of 1953—and since then he had been an Audrey fan. Certainly, Jacqueline Kennedy was in the Audrey mold. They were around the same height, weight, and coloring, and had similar figures. Their sense of fashion was the same— French designers were Jackie's favorites, too. Even their voices sounded similar, although Jackie's lacked Audrey's distinctive accent and lilt.

Kennedy's 1962 birthday celebration had taken place at Madison Square Garden amid an explosion of publicity caused by Marilyn Monroe performing her notorious "Happy Birthday, Mr. President" routine. She died shortly after, and the tremors caused by her death were still being felt.

This year's birthday fest was a somewhat toned-down affair. And it would be JFK's final birthday.

⌒•⌒

Weeks of rehearsals preceded the start date of *My Fair Lady*, to be followed by a four-month shooting schedule with days starting at 5:30 a.m. and ending at 9:00 p.m. Cast and crew dealt with the discomfort and upkeep of period costumes and wigs and enormous sets requiring ultrahot lights. It would be organized chaos. Filming would take place entirely in Hollywood rather than the studios in Europe where Audrey felt at home. It was far easier for Warners to monitor costs and production problems on its home turf for such a production. There was a different rhythm to shooting abroad. Audrey loved tea breaks during the day. That practice didn't exist in America. "You have to remember, I'm a European," she told a reporter, to Warners' consternation. Most Americans thought of Audrey as American.

For many, her singing caused a big controversy: the fact was, although she had sung a bit on film, she was not a singer. Would her voice be dubbed? Of course not. Audrey would do all of her own singing in *My Fair Lady*. As everyone knew, she had sung in *Sabrina*, had sung and danced with Fred Astaire in *Funny Face*, and had a smash hit with "Moon River" in *Breakfast at Tiffany's*. "'Moon River' was written for her," noted Henry Mancini. "No one else has ever understood it so completely. There have been more than a thousand versions of 'Moon River,' but hers is unquestionably the greatest." But nothing she had done musically required the tour-de-force, multi-octave soprano required for the score of *My Fair Lady*. Julie Andrews had been a unique discovery. For those who saw her in *My Fair Lady*, Audrey among them, it had been an unforgettable experience. "I must play Eliza," Audrey said at the time.

No question that Audrey could deliver the performance and the screen presence. But the singing? "I Could Have Danced All Night" was not "La Vie en Rose" or "Moon River." Still, she felt confident that she could do it. The whole endeavor was a striking example of how Machiavellian Hollywood could be. A great conspiracy was in progress at the highest levels—from Jack Warner to director George Cukor. From day one, Audrey had been under the impression she would do her own singing. But from the start, musical director André Previn made it clear to the studio that Audrey's voice would have to be dubbed.

There are those who moan that her voice should have been utilized somehow, that it would have provided an extra jolt of vérité, saved her the embarrassment of being dubbed, and would have resulted in a better film. However, her practice tracks, on which Audrey herself is singing the *My Fair Lady* songs, have since emerged. Her rendition of "I Could Have Danced All Night" was undeniably beyond her singing capabilities. Expecting singing lessons to provide what was lacking in Audrey's voice would be equivalent to asking a recreational ice skater, adept at skating around the rink and doing a spin or two, to be taught triple jumps—assuming she had the capacity to perform them—in a couple of months, and then to compete in and win a world championship immediately afterward.

Audrey faced another kind of ordeal: her diplomatic skills would be on high alert throughout the entire production. She had leading man Rex Harrison to contend with. Unlike Bill Holden, he wasn't in love with her. Like Cary Grant, he zealously protected his own turf. He was not pleased that he was being paid less than one-fifth of Audrey's salary. But he was respectful, and cautious not to treat Audrey in "bloody newcomer" fashion, as he had Julie Andrews.

She faced a monumental challenge in dealing with the film's costume, set, and scenery designer Cecil Beaton, who had also designed the stage production. He was a temperamental genius who wasn't on friendly terms with director Cukor. Audrey was caught in the middle. When disputes arose, each man expected her to take his side. There was a reason for the animosity between them. Beaton had long ago come close to marrying Greta Garbo—the ultimate marriage of convenience for both of them, as their sexual preferences ran the gamut. Cukor had talked her out of it. Beaton would never forget or forgive Cukor's meddling. Beaton referred to Cukor as "the little man." And the director's insistence on having his own production designer, Gene Allen, on this film, didn't help the relationship between Cukor and Beaton. Allen, who would be instrumental in translating Beaton's designs into actual sets, would receive credit on a separate title card. Temper tantrums from each man would erupt. Miraculously, Audrey managed to remain neutral. Beaton was fanatical on every detail regarding Audrey's appearance—costumes, hairstyles, even her eyelashes—and he was constantly making changes. She was relying on Cukor to guide her through a characterization that was turning out to be much more difficult than anticipated.

Cukor was under great pressure to deliver a masterpiece, which included strict instructions to remain absolutely true to the stage production. "No surprises in the screening room," declared Jack Warner. That shackled Cukor to a conventional, filmed rendition of the stage show, a far cry from his highly cinematic achievement with Judy Garland's *A Star Is Born,* also, coincidentally, a costly Warner Bros. picture.

Production of *My Fair Lady* remained a cauldron of troubles. The plum role that actresses would kill for turned into hard labor for Audrey, as filming lumbered along during one of the hottest summers on record in Southern California. Not a good time for serious personal problems to intrude.

Based on preview screenings, *Charade* was certain to be a hit. The publicity generated by teaming Audrey with Cary Grant was major.

But what of *Paris When It Sizzles?* Paramount had millions invested, and with Audrey, *Charade,* and *My Fair Lady* often in the news, it made sense for the studio to try to cash in on Audrey's high visibility. Bill's visibility had dropped to a new low.

The studio had come up with a slogan for the film.

Chapter

10

"HOLDEN AND HEPBURN GO ABSOLUTELY APE IN *Paris When It Sizzles*."

That was the marketing strategy, and the slogan decided on to sell the picture. Holden agreed to do prerelease publicity. As he had said, he considered it an important part of his job, but Audrey, for the most part, was unavailable. Not only was she mired in *My Fair Lady,* the word on *Paris* was not good. Distancing oneself from a potential flop has always been a wise tactical approach in Hollywood.

It's notable that when it came to their work, neither Audrey nor Bill sidestepped questions from the press. When Bill, interviewed on television in Britain, was asked what his favorite film was, he didn't fire off any glib responses, along the lines of, "I love them all, it's like asking who's your favorite child." Instead, he deliberated for a moment, then replied: "*Sunset Boulevard.* Billy Wilder, Gloria Swanson, Von Stroheim. I'd say that was my favorite film." And there was no mention of the slew of other hits that audiences identified him with, including *Sabrina.* Audrey took a similar approach. She treated reporters' questions seriously and gave thoughtful answers—sometimes too thoughtful and revealing, as far as whatever studio she was working for was concerned. Perhaps Paramount was better off not having Audrey talk about *Paris When It Sizzles.*

In the end, the film had not only *not* rekindled their romance; the former lovers wouldn't have the satisfaction of having a final hit together. The film had some bright moments, but though it was filled with frantic, talky action, it was dull and lacked true momentum. At the time, it was known in the industry as *Paris When It Fizzles*. The classic cinema adage held true: the greatest stars cannot salvage a turkey. *Lady L* suffered the same fate, as would, shortly, Charles Chaplin's über-flop, *A Countess from Hong Kong*. Chaplin, Marlon Brando, Sophia Loren, and Hitchcock discovery "Tippi" Hedren couldn't save it.

For future film buffs, some of whom would regard *Paris* as a lost treasure, one is reminded of George Cukor's comments regarding Greta Garbo's last film, *Two-Faced Woman,* which he directed. It was a critical and box-office failure. Years afterward, when told how "good" it was, Cukor adamantly disagreed: "Well, I think it's lousy. The script was bad—not funny. We all knocked ourselves out, but it just wasn't funny. That's the whole story."

While Audrey had made it clear to her agent, Kurt Frings, that re-teaming her with Bill in any further films was to be avoided, one never knew. She remained concerned about him. She had once wanted to marry him, have children with him. When they'd been in love, in the *Sabrina* days, his adoration had filled her heart with joy. He'd been protective, warm, kind, passionate. And he still adored her. She did not want to see him drunk all the time

Thanks to Capucine, the latest on Bill—how he was doing, what he was doing—would usually find its way into their conversations.

∽•⌣

Capucine was excited, anticipating a cruise. It was Sam Spiegel's idea. The P. T. Barnum/Flo Ziegfeld–like producer of Bill's *Bridge on the River Kwai* (among other great films, including *Lawrence of Arabia* and

The African Queen) was a key player on the international movie scene. He made a grand gesture: he offered his friends Bill and Cap his yacht, the fifty-ton *Malahane,* complete with crew and master chef, for a fantasy cruise. Only the lovebirds, no other guests.

Bill wanted this relationship to work. Capucine made him happy. Thanks to her, he was (for now) able to remain sober, and he appreciated all she had done for him. He did not want to throw away the happiness they could still enjoy together. As he once noted, "I like to get in a situation that is real, where I can say, 'Here's a chance to react as a human being, not some windup doll or robot that goes round and round a track.'"

Cap was doing her best to understand him better. Nonetheless, she was nervous and constantly on edge when they embarked on their romantic odyssey, always alert to anything that might set him off and lead to that first drink.

All agreed that Cap more than deserved this marvelous interlude. The things she'd had to put up with, the binges, Bill's periods of retreat from human contact. Bill felt guilty about all of it and hoped to make it up to her. But after two weeks of being alone with Cap with only the crew and the high seas for company, Holden grew moody and restive. If there had been doubts in his mind about marrying her, apparently this voyage confirmed them. By the time the yacht reached Barbados, their romance was over, although their relationship wasn't. Specifics on what caused Bill's change of heart were not forthcoming.

To Capucine's disappointment and dismay, there was no longer any doubt: Holden was not looking to cast her to replace the current Mrs. Holden. The best Audrey could do was to console her depressed friend. Years later, asked if Holden had been about to divorce Ardis to marry her, Capucine replied: "That would never have happened." Thanks to changing times, Bill could more or less openly carry on affairs without ever dissolving his marriage. It would take more than another woman, or a studio, or any agent's disapproval, to spell finis to the Holden marriage, now in its twenty-fifth year. Outsiders could not comprehend how this was possible (twenty-five years!), though insiders had long since accepted it. Some even admired them. Comedian Henny Youngman once joked that the secret of getting along with one's wife was simple: "Don't spend any time with her." It seemed to work for Ardis and Bill.

Bill's career seemed on the verge of a renaissance. John Madden, a reporter for *Variety* and a film buff, regarded a Holden comeback as inevitable. It all depended on when the right part came his way. "He was too highly regarded as an actor and a star to be written off, even at his lowest point. His romantic leading man days were almost over, but there was always more to his appeal than that." Bill had once described himself as the kind of guy that any other ordinary man could identify with: "If Holden can do it, the man thinks, then I can do it too." He viewed his talent much as Audrey viewed hers: "I'm a limited talent," noted Holden, "not a great actor. My forte always has been playing a kind of contemporary character that the audience can sympathize with."

Producer Jennings Lang has explained: "It's all about proper casting— if you have the right role for a star, you cast him, or her, even if they'd had a string of flops. Because casting is 95 percent of the game; if an actor is cast properly, you're likely to win the crapshoot, which is what making movies is all about." But casting a star with a serious drinking problem, who has also had recent flops, certainly compounds a producer's dilemma.

∽•⌒

Audrey's marriage seemed to be following in the footsteps of the Bill-and-Cap fiasco. Filming *Paris When It Sizzles* must have seemed like carefree months in the country compared to what Audrey was going through with *My Fair Lady* in the fall of 1963. Even contending with Bill, four-sheets-to-the-wind, had been a pleasure compared to this.

Those working on the film were aware of heated arguments between Audrey and Mel, which often went into high gear and could be heard by anyone in the vicinity of her dressing room. Publicist Max Bercutt worked overtime on damage control. Warners had gone all-out in providing Audrey with every star-perquisite on the list. The Beverly Hills residence they rented for her was the ultimate in luxury. At her request, her dressing room at the studio was surrounded by a white picket fence, complete with a "Positively Do Not Disturb" sign on the front gate.

But it was Mel, it seemed, who was causing the major disturbance in her life. He was desperately trying to launch several projects, with no success. It was a classic *Star Is Born*–like dilemma. Everyone wanted Audrey for their productions, but few were interested in Mel's projects if Audrey wasn't attached to them. It wasn't her fault—and it was understandable that Mel felt thwarted as far as his own ambitions were concerned. However: "You can't share talent," as Ava Gardner once observed about Frank Sinatra.

There was a film Mel wanted to do with Audrey: *Isabella of Spain.* But for Audrey, this was the worst time imaginable to have to deal with these matters, not to mention the latest stories she was hearing about Mel's womanizing. He'd always been discreet, but that wasn't necessarily the case with his inamoratas. A friend of Pat Gaston Manville's, a beautiful brunette dancer, had had an occasional rendezvous with Ferrer during his first marriage. She told Pat that Mel was a typical Latin lover. "Fernando Lamas was the same type," noted Pat. "Once, in Rome, I met Fernando at a party. He wanted me to go home with him. He was married to Arlene Dahl at the time, who was drop-dead gorgeous. 'What do you want with me when you've got her at home?' I asked. He went crazy. 'Why do you bring *her* up?' He went on and on. That's how they think, dear. A roll in the hay has nothing to do with the wife at home."

Bogged down in *Fair Lady*, Audrey needed every bit of Mel's support and love; she depended on him. But soon he would begin filming his role in *Sex and the Single Girl*. Tony Curtis, Natalie Wood, Henry Fonda, and Lauren Bacall headed the star-studded cast, and Mel was happy to get the job.

Because of the negative buzz regarding Audrey's singing, an extraordinarily ill advised idea was proposed: why not have her sing, informally, a couple of the *My Fair Lady* songs for gathered cast and crew? That would demonstrate once and for all that there was not going to be any problem with her singing. Audrey experienced firsthand, and perhaps for the first time, the meaning of the term "flop sweat."

She was smoking a couple of packs of cigarettes a day. As filming progressed, despite the countless times Rex Harrison had performed his role onstage, he began having trouble remembering dialogue, while Audrey always knew her lines perfectly. Many takes were necessary, on many occasions, calling on Audrey to display incredible stamina. Her resolve was remarkable, but the process was exhausting. She disliked her acting in the Cockney scenes and, for the first time in her career, gave in to bouts of temperament. She shocked Cukor by stopping in the middle of scenes (the ultimate insult—only the director could "stop" a scene), exclaiming that she thought she was doing a bad job. There were tantrums, complete with tears.

There were no such problems when it came to filming the Ascot races sequence, which was superbly designed and staged, with Audrey jaw-droppingly gorgeous in a Beaton fantasy creation. And the sequence revealing Eliza's final transformation into a lady, descending the stairs in Professor Higgins's home, breathtakingly gowned, bejeweled, and coiffed for the Royal Ball—those were the times that Audrey felt completely in her element. In these scenes, she was, once again, portraying a shimmering Cinderella, the essence of aristocratic elegance, glamour, and beauty, worth every penny of her million-dollar salary.

The time arrived when Warners' veteran music-department head Ray Heindorf met with Jack Warner and informed him that none of Audrey's music tracks could be used in the final film, except for "Just You Wait," and phrases here and there, of other songs. The task of telling Audrey was Warner's, who assigned a lesser mortal to deliver the news (the mogul was famous for avoiding such scenes with his stars). When told they were not using her voice, Audrey left the set and went home. The next day, she returned and apologized, but she was so upset that even Givenchy, who came to see her, could not lighten her mood.

Another Audrey "first" occurred: she now insisted that black screens be placed strategically on the set, so she wouldn't have to be distracted by the technical crew. At the same time, ever-more-sensitive Audrey tried to assuage any hurt feelings by hosting a special screening for cast and crew of *Charade*.

When she insisted that studio photographers be barred from the set—the clicking of their cameras was highly disturbing—the front office reminded her that their coverage of daily shooting was essential. She asked then that they wear black and be positioned behind the black screens, out of her sight line.

There were only two visitors permitted on the set: Givenchy and Doris Kleiner Brynner (the second wife of Yul Brynner). When baby Sean ran a fever, Audrey worried that her child's life was in mortal danger. Her pet canary flew the coop, and despite heavy security at the studio, her diamond wedding ring was stolen.

It was the first time in her career that so much seemed to be working against her. At least she had Assam of Assam, Mr. Famous's adorable successor, to dispense unconditional love.

The inevitable happened—Audrey collapsed. Production shut down, at great expense, so she could have several days of complete, undisturbed rest. Now that the end of filming was in sight, she wanted it to continue. It was a distraction from her troubled marital situation. However, a shock was in store. It had nothing to do with Mel, marriage, Cap, Bill, or *My Fair Lady*. On November 22, 1963, during filming on the Covent Garden set, there was calamitous news: JFK had been shot. Before notifying cast and crew, Cukor had an assistant verify the information, which turned out to be worse than expected. The president was dead.

Who would make the announcement? Audrey said she would do it, and she struggled to maintain her composure as she announced what had occurred. Her remarks were brief and heartfelt, and it was a profoundly sad moment. Jack Warner wanted filming to continue for the rest of the day, but the company disbanded. A pall hung over the remainder of production, which wrapped just before Christmas.

In an attempt to save her marriage, Audrey made a remarkable effort. She spent most of the next year constantly by Mel's side, traveling with him throughout Europe—she spoke Spanish, French, Dutch-Flemish, and Italian—as he pursued his own dreams.

The international film community was still only a small town in terms of industry gossip. Capucine and Bill Holden had remained friends, and when Bill heard about what was going on with the Ferrers, he was concerned and wanted to know how Audrey was doing. She was doing what she felt necessary to salvage her relationship with Mel.

Ferrer starred in a minor film about the Spanish artist El Greco and worked on an independent production of his own. Industry observers could not come up with another example of a star of Audrey's magnitude casting aside her career to physically help her husband make a movie in which she was not appearing. She performed jobs normally assigned to apprentice assistants. Hotel accommodations were third-rate, a far cry from the luxurious facilities she was accustomed to (although she drove a small car, a Volvo, and was no stranger to flying economy class). But Audrey had never forgotten the hard times she suffered during World War II, and she was still capable of roughing it.

Their social life was far from what could be considered roughing it. In Spain they were guests at a party given by the duchess of Alba, a friend of Mel's. At the party was a beautiful and voluptuous sixteen-year-old singer and flamenco artist, Marisol (born Josefa Flores Gonzalez). She was already a star in Spain and Japan, having made many appearances on television and in Spanish films. She performed that evening, and both Mel and, supposedly, Audrey were entranced by her talent. Mel wanted to direct her in a movie. According to several of Hepburn's biographers, Audrey thought that a marvelous idea. One might speculate, however, that perhaps Audrey's thoughts were more along the lines of Ardis Holden's when Bill brought Audrey home for dinner. In true European fashion, Audrey went along with her husband's interest in Marisol, even bringing her to Paris so that her renowned Parisian hairdresser, Alexandre, could perform a makeover, preparing Marisol to look her best in front of the cameras.

"Can you imagine Elizabeth [Taylor], or [Marlene] Dietrich, or Tallulah [Bankhead], going along with something like that?" recalled an amused Bernard Drew many years later. "Tallulah would have smacked Marisol so hard that her head would have gone flying over Portugal!" But Audrey willingly became an integral behind-the-scenes participant in the movie, *Cabriola*, which was also the title of one of Marisol's hit songs. She had suggestions on the script and even offered directorial suggestions; industry scuttlebutt suggested it might have turned out better if Audrey had directed the whole movie.

~•⌒

Hollywood could be a nasty, vengeful little town. *My Fair Lady* was nominated for Academy Awards in virtually every category, including Best Picture, Best Actor, Best Director. But Audrey had had the effrontery to snatch the leading role from the young woman most people felt was entitled to play it; how dare she? Dubbed singing voice and all, Hollywood was not going to reward her. She wasn't nominated. And the voice behind Audrey, Marni Nixon, made a major mistake by letting it be known that she was the singing voice of Eliza. She was blacklisted in the industry for years.

After a decade of nothing but goodwill toward Audrey, suddenly she was on the receiving end of hostile personal comments. There was no love lost for Jack Warner, either, and the fact that the picture was proving to be a big hit was deeply annoying to Tinseltown's artistic community. The mogul's gamble on Audrey had paid off. "Jack wasn't going to take any chance on turning over *My Fair Lady* to unproven talent, which Julie Andrews was as a screen personality at the time. He wasn't about to produce a $17 million screen test for a newcomer," said Charles ("Charlie") Einfeld, Warner's longtime publicity chief.

It seemed Julie Andrews might have the last laugh after all. She was nominated for the Best Actress Oscar for her debut film, Walt Disney's *Mary Poppins*. It, too, was a big hit and at a substantially lower production cost than *My Fair Lady*. Andrews unquestionably had the overwhelming support of those who would vote in the Oscar derby. Audrey would not be attending the ceremonies. Why should she appear, feed the controversy, and boost ratings for the Oscar-cast when her work had been overlooked? George Cukor begged her to attend, arguing that the town's hatred for Jack Warner was responsible for the snub. Incredibly, she honestly thought her performance simply had not warranted a nomination. If she had done the proper job, she said, all else aside, she would have been nominated.

Cooler heads prevailed. It made sense for Audrey to attend and not appear to be ashamed or embarrassed. Furthermore, why not have Audrey present the Best Actor Oscar? If Harrison won, there would be photos all over the world of the two of them together, Audrey presenting the Oscar to co-star Rex. A win for *My Fair Lady* no matter what.

Julie Andrews, weeks earlier, had won the Golden Globe over Audrey for Best Actress, for *Mary Poppins*. Andrews later said she realized that if she had done the film of *My Fair Lady*, she wouldn't have been available to do *Mary Poppins*. So in her acceptance speech she thanked Jack Warner ("He laughed, thank God," recalled Andrews).

Building up a rivalry between Hepburn and Andrews guaranteed great copy in the days leading up to the Oscar show, on April 5, 1965, at the Santa Monica Civic Auditorium. Audrey had flown in from Europe especially for the event. Toward the end of the evening, host Bob Hope included no humorous asides when he announced, to present the Best Actor award, "Ladies and gentlemen, the always gracious and wonderful Audrey Hepburn!" Walking to center stage, she looked spectacular, dressed in the perfect Givenchy gown.

She read the list of nominees: Richard Burton for *Becket*, Peter O'Toole for *Becket*, Anthony Quinn for *Zorba the Greek*, Rex Harrison for *My Fair Lady*, and Peter Sellers for *Dr. Strangelove: Or How I Learned to Stop Worrying and Love the Bomb*. She paused, tore open the envelope, flashed the ultimate Hepburn smile, gazed directly at the audience and announced: "The winner is—Rex Harrison!"

There was thunderous applause as Harrison came up onstage and gave Audrey a long hug. She handed him the statuette. Then, in a most unusual move—prearranged, in the event Harrison won—Audrey continued to stand alongside Rex as he delivered his acceptance speech, his arm around her waist, clutching Oscar in his free hand. He glanced over at Audrey, and concluded with: "I feel I should split it in half."

A slightly bewildered-looking Julie Andrews was seated in the audience close to the stage as Harrison looked her way, and said: "My deep love to two fair ladies."

My Fair Lady was also awarded Best Picture, and George Cukor won Best Director. "I'm very grateful, very happy, and very lucky," he said. His nemesis, Cecil Beaton, won for Best Costume Design. Andrews won the Oscar for Best Actress that night, and Audrey was first to congratulate her.

Bill's movies were no longer Oscar-caliber; the projects were far from those of the "Golden Holden" years. He wasn't interested in attending the many film festivals that had sprung up, especially those where *Sabrina* would be a highlight because of interest in Bogart, who was highly popular with nostalgia buffs. Audrey, too, bypassed these occasions.

Financially, Bill had no worries. He'd always been a shrewd businessman and was worth several million dollars. Bill's life wasn't that of a once-great star living a solitary existence in a small apartment, alone with his press clippings. "If only he'd been able to stop the drinking, he'd have remained in huge demand by all the top producers and directors," noted Blake Edwards, who would work with Bill in the future. But, although there would be periods of sobriety, Bill would always crawl back into "that awful, black cave."

Chapter

11

Iᴛ's *ɴᴏᴛ* ᴏᴠᴇʀ, ᴅᴇᴄɪᴅᴇᴅ Aᴜᴅʀᴇʏ. Fᴏʀ ᴛʜᴇ sᴀᴋᴇ ᴏғ ᴛʜᴇɪʀ child, and a horror at joining her mother in the ranks of divorcées, Audrey would continue to be Mrs. Mel Ferrer; she would not give up on the marriage. They would somehow work things out. There was still something left in him that she loved, and she yearned for another baby.

She took great joy in their new home, located in Tolochenaz, a municipality in the canton of Vaud, on the shores of Lake Geneva in western Switzerland. The French-speaking population numbered under 2,000. The Ferrers christened their new domicile La Paisible (the peaceful place). The sixteenth-century, two-story, nine-bedroom stone farmhouse would be transformed by Audrey into a subtly luxurious and comfortable oasis of peace and tranquillity for her family. It would remain her permanent residence.

For Mel, there were few requests for his services as actor, writer, or director. Although offers for Audrey were always plentiful, Mel remained on the hunt for uniquely suitable projects for her. The idea to team her again with Cary Grant, for a remake of *Goodbye, Mr. Chips,* fell through. Audrey as Peter Pan came close, but legal complications over rights to the title prevented it from moving forward. Other projects remained possibilities, including an original script by novelist Frederic Raphael, *Two for the Road;* and a film of *Wait Until Dark,* the suspense play by Frederick Knott.

There was no longer any threat from Hedda, Louella, Sheilah, *Confidential* (which had gone out of business), or any other journalistic enterprise with the power to shatter careers. Extramarital affairs were now not only tolerated but, in some circles, celebrated. At thirty-six, Audrey was not immune to a new relationship, if the right opportunity presented itself. When times were tough, she was vulnerable. Late in his life, Billy Wilder reflected on this aspect of Hepburn's persona: "Audrey was something entirely different on the screen than what she was in real life. Not that she was vulgar—she wasn't . . . But there was so much inside her and she could put the sexiness on a little bit and the effect was really something."

For Audrey, her safest habitat remained the screen, and once again she went back to the protective cocoon of big-time moviemaking.

William Wyler had called. Her last picture with him, *The Children's Hour,* had failed. But Willie had discovered her, made her a star. It was under his direction that she had won her Oscar. She trusted him and would always be grateful to him. She would never turn down an opportunity to work with him, and there was always that possibility they would come up with another *Roman Holiday.* Willy's new project sounded great. *How to Steal a Million,* a caper film, would combine theft, romance, glamour, suspense, and fun—not unlike *Charade,* which is undoubtedly how the package was sold to 20th Century-Fox. Wyler, at sixty-five, was still at the top of his profession; he would soon direct Barbra Streisand in the film version of *Funny Girl.* But the toll on mind and body was profound. Wyler's wife, Talli, later recalled how when making a film her husband thought of nothing else.

How to Steal a Million would be made in Paris, with Audrey portraying the daughter of a successful art forger. Her leading man would be Lawrence of Arabia himself, Peter O'Toole, in the role of a suave burglar who falls in love with her. O'Toole's acting pedigree was impeccable. He had attended the Royal Academy of Dramatic Arts on a scholarship and was besotted with the theater. Very tall, slim, Irish, classically handsome, and sexy, in an aristocratic way, he would undoubtedly look great paired with Audrey on-screen. O'Toole knew all of Shakespeare's sonnets, considered himself a romantic, and was nervous at the prospect of being Audrey's leading man. From what he'd heard, she was aloof and formal.

Her trusted cameraman, Charles Lang, and Alberto and Grazia De Rossi, in charge of makeup and hair, would ensure that Audrey looked wonderful. Givenchy would be creating her wardrobe. At one point, for plot purposes, Audrey would be outfitted as a scrubwoman. "That does it," says O'Toole, in character, observing Audrey's discomfort. "Does what?" she asks. "It gives Givenchy a night off," he replies.

The $6-million budget guaranteed top-of-the-line production values. George Bradshaw and Hollywood veteran Harry Kurnitz wrote the script for what all anticipated to be a big hit. The supporting cast was stellar—Hugh Griffith, Eli Wallach, and Charles Boyer. There was chemistry between Audrey and O'Toole. Aloof and formal Audrey was not—his riveting blue eyes, cultured voice, and skill as an actor were irresistible. He was certainly attracted to her. But during production, in the fall of 1965, she learned she was pregnant. Against the advice of her doctors, she told no one, including director Wyler. She felt a new affection for Mel, who was very loving and attentive during this period.

The visual impact of Audrey, in a scene in which she wears a ravishing black-lace cocktail dress (with matching mask!), spark-lit by Cartier diamond earrings and glitter on her eyelids, was mesmerizing and memorable. The way she looked was "a veritable definition of star quality," wrote one critic. The film was a visual feast. Audrey—and Paris—had never been more beautiful, and Hepburn looked a decade younger than her thirty-six years. Only the script was routine and predictable.

In advertising, publicity, and promotion on the picture, Audrey's wardrobe was treated as one of the stars. The marketing strategy for the film was not all that different from *Paris When It Sizzles,* bursting with innuendo: the preview trailer begins with a shot of O'Toole asking Audrey: "You really want it that much?" "More!" she replies. The announcer chimes in: "Only Audrey Hepburn could make him do it! Only Peter O'Toole could do it! Only three-time Academy Award–winning director William Wyler could show Hepburn and O'Toole, the screen's greatest new romantic team, how to do it!" The public was interested, but not overwhelmingly so. The screen's "greatest new romantic team" did not make another film together.

∼•〇

Sean would have a sibling at last, an answered prayer for Audrey after her tragic miscarriage a few years earlier. But, sadly, in December she suffered another miscarriage, and it left her desolate. The only thing to do was to return to work.

Audrey's new leading man reminded her in many ways of a another co-star. Without any overt physical resemblance to Bill Holden, Albert Finney did possess his qualities of virility, sensitivity, sense of humor, and sense of fun. She was ready for another Holden, and there was no Mrs. Finney to contend with—he was divorced.

Finney, along with Peter O'Toole, was among the hottest young actors on the international film scene (the two actors had been class-mates at the Royal Academy of Dramatic Arts). Charles Laughton had labeled Finney "a genius." Producer-director Stanley Donen had scored a coup by signing him to be Audrey's leading man in *Two for the Road*. He'd been a sensation in the title role of Tony Richardson's ribald Best Picture Oscar winner, *Tom Jones*. For the moment, Finney was a sex symbol as well as a respected actor. Audrey and "Albie" made a slightly odd-looking couple. Finney was five feet nine, barely two inches taller than Hepburn (O'Toole had been well over six feet). O'Toole was three years younger than Audrey; Finney, seven years.

Two for the Road would be Audrey's third film with Donen (after *Funny Face* and *Charade*). To her delight, her beloved Paris would be their home base, with partial filming to take place in the South of France. The script, by novelist Frederic Raphael, was very European in flavor. It was his follow-up effort to *Darling*, which had garnered two 1965 Oscars—Best Screenplay for him, and Best Actress for Julie Christie as the title character.

Two for the Road was an ambitious, fiercely contemporary story that, for Audrey, struck close to home. It followed one couple's love, marriage, and infidelities over the course of a twelve-year period. A little too close, perhaps; it took a lot of convincing from Donen and Raphael for her to feel comfortable with it. There was an additional, major drawback, which did not seem to concern anyone: the two leading characters were rather unlikable, just as Raphael's characters in *Darling* had been.

Audrey's character would run the gamut from the late teen years to her current age. Makeup and hair gurus Alberto and Grazia De Rossi would once again be invaluable in helping her to achieve her various looks for this film. Although she looked younger than her age, it was difficult to make the scenes where she was supposed to be in her late teens convincing.

Audrey would not have the "protection" of a Givenchy wardrobe, a major concern for her; again, a lot of discussion was required. (Mel was not unhappy; he was still not a Givenchy fan). Although Donen had memorialized Audrey as a fashion icon in *Funny Face,* he had no intention of revisiting that territory in the same way. A fashion revolution was underway, and he wanted Audrey to be in the forefront. The turning point had been recent. To quote society chronicler William Norwich, "there's a New Look in town, and her name is Barbra Streisand. . . ." At the beginning of her career, Streisand had been strongly influenced by Audrey's look in *Breakfast at Tiffany's.* Now, the twenty-three-year-old singer, and the way she dressed, was, to quote Norwich, "a big idea whose time has come." "Throwaway Chic" was the future.

Donen wanted Audrey totally "real" in this film. It would be ridiculous for the character she was playing—a touring choir girl when she first meets her aspiring architect future husband—to wear Givenchy couture. Audrey finally agreed, worked diligently with fashion coordinator Ken Scott, and literally wore him out with her surgeonlike dedication to assembling her "off-the-rack" costumes. When Lady Clare Rendlesham came aboard, it was exhausting for her, too; in fact, exhausting for all but Audrey, who was totally committed to familiarizing herself with the boutique fashions of the "in" designers, including Mary Quant and Paco Rabanne. She was to wear bathing suits on-screen for the first time and that made her nervous, reluctant to put her body, with all its perceived flaws, under that kind of scrutiny. Donen was a very persuasive man. There was a discreet nude love scene, in which Donen did not want Audrey to wear a flesh-colored bodysuit; once again, he prevailed.

The structure of the film was unlike anything she had ever appeared in, with continual intercutting between past and present. It was a thoroughly daunting but challenging project that required all of Audrey's attention and sparked her enthusiasm.

Especially for her leading man.

~•~

Albert Finney later said that he met Audrey in what he described as a "seductive ambiance" in "a very sensual time in the Mediterranean." It was as though he were channeling Bill Holden when he recalled, "We got on immediately. After the first day's rehearsals [with Holden, too, it had been the first day], I could tell the relationship would work out wonderfully."

Certainly, Audrey's anxieties over Mel seemed to fade. There was more than an echo of her early Holden days as she and Finney, dressed as two ordinary young people, laughed and held hands while walking along the shores of the Loire. They took drives to out-of-the-way cafés and boîtes (small nightclubs) where they could dine, dance, and enjoy each other. Except for the fact that these forays took place not in the hills of Hollywood but in the South of France, it was Holden redux. Exactly as she had with Bill, Audrey permitted herself to be a "girl" again, unencumbered by the worries and cares that came with being Mrs. Mel Ferrer and Audrey Hepburn. Director Donen was delighted with this "new" Audrey—she was open to any and all ideas on how to play her role.

It was an intoxicating time for her. Her spirits soared again. She hoped "Albie" felt the same intimacy. With Bill, she'd had no doubt— of course, she was only twenty-five then. A lot of life had happened in the interim.

When the production schedule permitted, she flew to Switzerland to spend time with six-year-old son Sean. The Ferrers were both present when the boy performed in a school play, his parents nervously anticipating his debut as they sat together in the audience. Audrey was tickled when Sean followed her advice to the letter and spoke confidently in a loud voice so he would be heard—the same advice she had undoubtedly been given by Mel, over and over, during the runs of *Gigi* and *Ondine*.

As to future projects, Mel would be producing *Wait Until Dark*. After the success of *My Fair Lady*, Warners was eager to have Audrey in another film; it would be made in Hollywood, despite her protestations. Mel had not the slightest intention of letting the deal slip away, as his career was otherwise dormant. Hepburn would be paid in excess of $1 million, plus a percentage of the gross.

Although Mel was aware of reports linking Audrey and Finney romantically, he was the last person who could complain about anyone, least of all Audrey, having an affair. If industry scuttlebutt was accurate, he was currently having one with Marisol. Finney's commitments would keep him in Europe, though that did not have to mean the end of his love affair with Audrey. But there was another, crucial element influencing Audrey's decision to call it quits: her relationship with her son would be threatened if she didn't.

On-screen, oddly enough, Finney wasn't a perfect leading man for Audrey, although their attraction to each other certainly brought out an openness in her performance that was refreshing. But his voice and accent didn't complement hers; they seemed to be from different worlds. And both appeared to be working very hard at creating their characters (whereas, in a brief scene with young femme fatale Jacqueline Bisset, Finney was effortlessly on target). There was a reason Audrey had come off so well opposite Holden, Bogart, Peck, Grant, Harrison, and O'Toole. These men matched what she had to offer. It made sense that she was attracted to them, even if they, with the exception of O'Toole, were older. And in terms of men more her age, she was a good match, on-screen, with George Peppard in *Breakfast at Tiffany's,* as well.

In *Two for the Road*, Audrey was too innately poised and refined for her role, although many critics regarded it as her best work to date. Some of her friends, for example, Audrey Wilder, thought it was a genuine breakthrough, that Audrey had never been less guarded on-screen. But not only was the character Joanna not really likable, she was supposed to be an "ordinary" woman. Try as she might, Audrey simply wasn't ordinary, any more than she was a Cockney. And Finney, often described as the incarnation of the British working-class hero, was miscast as an architect.

The dialogue was ultracontemporary. For the first (and last) time, she said the word "bastard" on-screen (she says it, with a smile, to Finney); and Finney was the first man to call Hepburn a "bitch" on-screen. Nudity, foul language, and moral ambiguity were becoming commonplace in films. The drugs-and-sex generation was in the forefront. "Those days were all about youth, youth, youth," recalled Hepburn's contemporary and fellow Britisher Joan Collins. There were no Sabrinas to be discovered in this discontented group.

Audrey's willingness to enable a production to realize its full technical potential was never more evident than on this film. Henry Mancini was the number-one choice to write the score, but there was doubt whether his commitments would permit it. Audrey made a personal appeal to Mancini via telegram to be a part of their "wonderful project." She even included a telephone number where she could be reached. "Can you imagine Elizabeth Taylor doing something like that, giving a contact number?" laughed MCA executive Herb Steinberg, who had been at Paramount during Hepburn's Holden days. Audrey's telegram to Mancini accomplished its purpose. He wrote the score for *Two for the Road*.

A couple of years earlier, after Elizabeth Taylor had starred in a highly rated network television special, "Elizabeth Taylor in London," Audrey received a telegram from an independent producer asking if she would be interested in her own TV special, "Audrey Hepburn in Switzerland." The telegram outlined exactly what the producer had in mind, which would be to include brief clips from her films, and he included a list of those he wanted to use. He promptly received a reply from Audrey herself, thanking him but politely declining his proposal. In her telegram she pointed out: "But you forgot Gregory Peck and *Roman Holiday*."

∼•⌒

There was shocking news about Bill Holden. To Audrey, Capucine, and the others who had known him over the years, it seemed sadly inevitable that eventually he would have an accident and either kill himself or somebody else. He did the latter, driving under the influence (he said he'd had only two glasses of wine) at over one hundred miles per hour, in an automobile accident in Italy. Two young women, sisters, were with him in the car.

The accident occurred, ironically, at a time when Bill was striving to improve his health. He had checked into a favorite resort, the beautiful La Pace Spa in Montecatini Terme, Tuscany. There, under the supervision of doctors, he'd embarked on a fitness program that included a strict, supervised diet, hot baths, the works. At the spa, Bill had met the young women who were with him in the car. They were reportedly granddaughters of the noted American writer Anita Loos. They wanted to visit friends in a nearby village, not far from the spa. "I'll drive you," volunteered Bill. En route, his Ferrari collided with a small Fiat coming from the opposite direction. The driver of the Fiat was rushed to the hospital but died in the ambulance. Bill and the women were unharmed.

Holden was charged with vehicular manslaughter. It took over a year to settle the case, but in the end, an eight-month suspended prison sentence was the court verdict. "Oh, Bill," had become "Poor Bill." He was devastated, overwhelmed with guilt, and the feeling never went away for long. Fortunately, friends in high places liked and respected him. It was not public knowledge, and Holden would never discuss it, but during his extensive travels he had done work for the Central Intelligence Agency. Strategic strings were quietly pulled behind the scenes. Bill kept a very low profile during this period, and eventually fallout from the scandal dissipated, then disappeared.

The preceding couple of years had been very rough. Bill suffered a terrible loss when his brother, Dick, a pilot, was killed in a flying accident. His parents, living in retirement in Palm Springs, California, were bereft; he did his best to console them, and himself.

Thankfully, a new woman had entered Bill's life. At a New Year's Eve party at the home of screenwriter and close Billy Wilder pal Charles Lederer, he introduced himself to a comely blonde with a "Hi, I'm Bill." He was delighted to learn that she was not an actress. That fierce, ruthless drive, that sense of purpose, that all-consuming concern about career was not the prime factor in her life. Like Audrey, Patricia Morgan Stauffer had an upper-class background. Her family was socially prominent, and her father was a successful Los Angeles stockbroker. She had attended the finest schools, and at one point was a pre-med student at the University of Southern California. A former Anne Klein model, Pat was not a stranger to luminaries from the entertainment world. She was the fifth wife of Swiss-born restaurateur Teddy Stauffer, a former musician and bandleader, a man noted for being a connoisseur of beautiful women (two of his wives were famous actresses, Faith Domergue and Hedy Lamarr). "Teddy was quite a character," recalled Pat Gaston Manville. "He certainly knew how to have a good time." Teddy was the entrepreneur who had put Acapulco on the map as a jet-set attraction, hence his nickname, "Mr. Acapulco." He and Pat had a two-year old daughter, Melinda, but were in the process of getting a divorce.

Pat would be a part of Bill's life for the next seventeen years. Holden's travels and film work continued, and Pat often accompanied him on location and on his trips to Africa. In many ways Bill was lucky; besides his looks and talent, he always connected with a beautiful, intelligent, loving woman who did her best to help him overcome his addictions.

In 1967, Bill was appearing on-screen as one of the all-star cast of a James Bond film that didn't star Sean Connery, *Casino Royale*.

~•~

"Make Something Wonderful About Being Alive!" was the ad line for Audrey's *Two for the Road*. The public was interested, but not overly so; the film played Radio City Music Hall in New York City, and the combination of Hepburn and Finney, and Donen, was an international draw.

Audrey would have to fight two major battles regarding the upcoming *Wait Until Dark*. She was determined to get the film made in Europe, and although she would be playing a blind woman, she was determined to avoid wearing the incredibly uncomfortable contact lenses necessary to simulate the look. She felt she could accomplish that through her performance alone. She certainly had a powerful ally, or so she assumed, in Jack Warner, who was producing and had personally selected her to star in the film. Audrey had wanted Sean Connery for the leading man, but the role went to Efrem Zimbalist Jr., who was completing his Warner Bros. contract.

A question had arisen over whether the studio could secure proper insurance on Hepburn. Her health at this point was not robust, although no specifics were revealed. The situation was resolved.

Audrey's one and only choice to direct *Wait Until Dark* was the dashing Terence Young, with whom she had a unique personal connection.

During World War II, the Hepburn family had hidden him from German occupiers during the Battle of Arnhem in the Netherlands. Audrey had been fifteen at the time, and Young almost thirty. He was very tall and handsome, and was the son of the commissioner of the Shanghai Municipal Police. He had attended Cambridge. During the war he was a tank commander in the Irish Guards.

He had encountered Audrey at the very beginning of her film career in England and was impressed even then. He directed the initial James Bond films—*Dr. No; From Russia, with Love;* and *Thunderball*—and had been instrumental in fashioning Sean Connery's on-screen image as James Bond: "Terence was James Bond," wrote Bond-film biographer Robert Cotton. Young was sophisticated, impeccably dressed, witty, an expert on wines, and a person seemingly comfortable in any circumstance.

Audrey knew she would have Young's unqualified protection and support. When his current film commitment encountered production difficulties, it seemed he wouldn't be available to direct *Wait Until Dark*. Other suggestions were offered. Audrey's response: "We'll wait for Terry."

Just as Warners had insisted on with *My Fair Lady,* the studio was adamant that *Wait Until Dark* be made in Hollywood, where costs and production could be closely monitored (though there would be some location work in New York). Audrey seemed intransigent on this point, and the studio subsequently informed the Ferrers that not only would Warners not make the film in Europe, but, if she withdrew, there would be a lawsuit for costs to date—a huge sum, and Audrey's and Mel's agents would be included in that lawsuit. As a producer, Mel had let his star/wife down; however, there were major victories. Terence Young would direct, and filming hours would be European-style, noon to 8:00 p.m. (later adjusted, at Jack Warner's insistence, to 11:30 a.m. to 7:30 p.m.).

Warners made one additional concession to keep Audrey happy: an artificial English garden was created on the soundstage, where cast and crew could enjoy daily tea breaks. Tea breaks were Hepburn's—and Terence Young's—way of lessening the day's tensions. "It was either that or have a star on the rampage," wrote one columnist. But these weren't the 1950s; it didn't much matter what was written now, even about Audrey Hepburn. It mattered to her, of course, but she knew they were not paying her for anything other than her box office clout. She'd proven to be a champion in that arena for nearly fifteen consecutive years and had no desire or intention to continue indefinitely.

Audrey was determined to prove that contact lenses weren't necessary for her to portray the blind girl. With Young's encouragement, she studied harder than ever and consulted experts, as did he, to ensure an accurate portrayal of a woman who could not see.

Again there would be no Givenchy wardrobe. Audrey was portraying a woman of limited means who lived in a tiny Greenwich Village apartment. Warners assigned a strict budget for Audrey's boutique-bought clothes, and when costs went beyond that, Mel had to contend with the studio's refusal to pay. Furthermore, his own expenses came under scrutiny.

Production finally began, in New York City, during a numbingly cold January in 1967. The first rushes showed that, expert as Audrey's attempts were, those famous Hepburn eyes still appeared to the camera to be "seeing." She would have to wear the contact lenses. It was an enervating physical ordeal—putting in, taking out, and wearing those eye-irritating contacts for hours on end, day after day, while keeping her energy level where it had to be to play the scenes. It was almost as hard as getting through *My Fair Lady*. Tension between Audrey and Mel intensified. At least she had Terence to guide her and keep her spirits up on this difficult journey.

Chapter

12

IN 1967, AUDREY'S CLOSE FRIEND, DORIS BRYNNER, WAS IN the process of divorcing her husband Yul, who later said he wondered how Audrey could have put up with Mel for so long. He thought that Ferrer was "jealous of her success" and that she had done everything humanly possible to make things work. Brynner, a notorious womanizer, did not comment on why his wife was divorcing him. Did anyone have a happy marriage? Even the unmarrieds—Capucine and Bill Holden were a classic example—always seemed to have nothing but problems.

The Ferrers settled into their ultraluxe accommodations in a bungalow of the Beverly Hills Hotel, as production on *Wait Until Dark* progressed. While the freezing cold of New York in winter had been replaced by the eternal spring-summer of California, the climate change hardly alleviated the source of Audrey's unhappiness. The couple's marriage was unraveling day by day, but the movie was turning out well. The make-believe world of the soundstage had become Audrey's temporary reality. It was the real world that seemed a fantasy.

According to studio sources, the casting couch was apparently getting a workout as Mel decided on which actress would portray a dead woman in a key scene of *Wait Until Dark*. Audrey was aware of this but had no choice other than to somehow retain her emotional and physical equilibrium as production approached its final phase. After that, it could very well be a final good-bye to Mel. In interviews she gave during this period, she told reporters that her marriage was in great shape, and wasn't it amazing? They had been together fourteen years! Her statements were not challenged to her face. In print, it was a different story.

There were lighthearted moments on the set. Audrey and the cast—including Alan Arkin, Jack Weston, and Richard Crenna—liked each other, and there were playful practical jokes to alleviate the tension. Audrey laughed a lot. The fact that she couldn't often clearly see her co-stars because of the contacts made it all the more difficult, but everyone marveled at her built-in resilience, which was quite remarkable.

She was overjoyed by a visit from seven-year-old Sean over his Easter break. The boy was accustomed to living and going to school in Switzerland. Trips to Disneyland and other tourist attractions with her son were a highlight for them both, and to her relief, she wasn't besieged by autograph hounds.

Her work in *Wait Until Dark* was turning out to be outstanding. She was creating a character who, as one reviewer would point out, was at the same time feminine, fragile, and independent: "She never lets one feel sorry for her character." It was a subtle, powerful achievement, which would be rewarded with an Oscar nomination. Despite all the problems and personal angst, the film came in under budget, and Henry Mancini would compose the musical score.

∾•◠

Audrey's final attempt to lower the hysteria and salvage her marriage was dramatic: She was pregnant again. And once again, she miscarried.

For all practical purposes, the marriage was finally over. She wanted Mel to plead for her forgiveness. She felt betrayed and depressed. The fact that Mel was going to produce a new version of *Mayerling,* starring not Audrey but France's young blonde goddess, Catherine Deneuve, was another blow—one compounded when she learned that Terence Young would be the director. Despite being Audrey's friend, apparently Young had gotten along well with Mel on *Wait Until Dark*. When *Mayerling* subsequently flopped, the reviews complained about the lack of chemistry between Deneuve and Omar Sharif, just as they had years ago with Audrey and Mel in their television version.

Wait Until Dark opened at New York's Radio City Music Hall. Standing at the rear of the vast Art Deco auditorium, which accommodated over 6,000 patrons, it was more than gratifying for the filmmakers to hear the hair-raising collective screams from the audience at the climactic moment when the villain, presumably just killed, springs to life and lunges at a blind-but-not-so-helpless Audrey. After the premiere, Universal executive Jerry Evans recalled seeing Audrey, together with Mel, Terence Young, and a Warner Bros. contingent, all smiling and congratulating each other as they left the theater. Evans spoke with one of his Warners pals, who said Warners expected the film to "go through the roof," which was good news for the studio. *Bonnie and Clyde*, released a couple of months earlier, was becoming a big hit for Warners. But that wasn't the case with the costly musical version of *Camelot;* Jack Warner had bypassed Julie Andrews once again. Vanessa Redgrave—another non singer!—was cast as Queen Guinevere, the role Andrews had created on the stage. The movie was a critical and box office failure. With *Wait Until Dark,* Hepburn had come through for him yet again, putting Warner in a great position to sell the studio that year.

The movie was a solid thriller and went on to gross a fortune throughout the world. Audrey's share was in the millions. She was remaining a first-magnitude star in a dramatically changing movie world—one that had changed greatly even since the recent *My Fair Lady.* This was the year not only of *Bonnie and Clyde* but also *The Graduate, Cool Hand Luke,* and *Guess Who's Coming to Dinner.* Faye Dunaway was the new star sensation. Her look in *Bonnie and Clyde,* as Audrey's had been after *Roman Holiday* and *Sabrina,* was a major influence on fashion. In Dunaway's case, according to some it was the "Poor Look."

Audrey flew to Hollywood to be a presenter at the Academy Awards—and, she hoped, to pick up her second Oscar—at the Santa Monica Civic Auditorium, on April 10, 1968. Grace Kelly, on film, made a special presentation regarding the foreign-film nominees; and Bill's film *Casino Royale* won Best Song (for "The Look of Love"). Ironically, Audrey lost the Oscar to the other Hepburn, Katharine, who won for *Guess Who's Coming to Dinner.* It was considered unlikely, however, that the younger Hepburn would ever issue a statement along the lines of Katharine's: "They don't usually give these things to the old girls, you know."

After that, around the same time she was initiating divorce proceedings, Audrey took a much-needed break. To her consternation, she was on her own—without a protector—and she didn't like it. She lost weight, and at one point she was a skeletal one hundred pounds.

She found distraction on Europe's social—very social—scene. She was in the fast lane, a cautious participant in la dolce vita. She generated her own field of energy, her own sex appeal. She made the acquaintance of a well-connected, titled woman who was, in effect, a matchmaker for the rich and famous, and with her help, started dating.

There was a renowned matador, Antonio Ordonez, seven years younger; the chemistry wasn't right. There was Prince Alfonso de Borbon y de Dampierre, a pretender to the Spanish throne and a world-class skier. If Mel, as reported, was angry on learning of Audrey's involvement with the prince, it only proved his dedication to the double standard.

Bitterness, unfortunately, was to characterize Mel and Audrey's feelings about each other. They didn't speak, except on urgent family matters, for over two decades. At one point, Audrey even denied Mel access to their son, albeit temporarily. An old adage accurately described Audrey at this point: "Don't look back—something might be gaining on you." She was disillusioned and deeply disappointed that her marriage was over.

One intense desire remained: to find another "Mr. Right," and to have another child. She was determined that Sean have a sibling. In less than two years, she would be forty. Her biological clock was running down.

Although the Spanish prince was a charmer, Audrey was not swept off her feet. She wasn't going to make any rash commitments, certainly not in the midst of her unpleasant divorce. It was proving to be a complex, drawn-out negotiation. A great deal of money, property, and investments were at stake.

PART III

Chasing Rainbows

Chapter

13

I F YOU'RE A MAN, AN ACTOR, AND OVER THE YEARS A CERTAIN toughness emerges in your performances, a result of the punches life has given you, you're admired for having 'matured,'" observed Billy Wilder. "I saw that toughness in Bill Holden's later movies. But if you're a beautiful woman, an actress, hit hard by life, and as you age that tough quality shows through, you're finished."

Bill's newfound hard edge had caught the interest of important younger directors. Although Audrey was tired, she was managing successfully to retain the qualities that made her so appealing. But both Audrey and Bill had by now learned a lesson as old as civilization. Success wasn't much fun. It had not been all they'd expected. Audrey was not sure what she expected. Happiness, probably—but wasn't that to be found in success? As actor-director Clint Eastwood noted, "When you're reaching for the brass ring, all you're thinking about is the brass ring."

She accepted an invitation. It came from friends, megawealthy French businessman Paul-Annik Weiller and his dazzling twenty-four-year-old Italian wife, Princess Olimpia Torlonia, a granddaughter of Queen Ena of Spain. (Weiller's father's first question to his blue-blooded daughter-in-law had been: "You are Italian. Can you cook pasta?") Audrey had briefly dated the princess's brother, Prince Marino Torlonia, a banker. He wasn't her cup of tea, but she saw eye to eye with Olimpia on the subject of motherhood (the Weillers would go on to have six children). She was happy to join the couple and a select group of their very rich friends on a cruise of the Greek Islands on the Weillers' immaculate yacht, complete with crew of sailors and a Cordon Bleu chef. "Who knows, Audrey, you might fall in love," said Paul Weiller.

Sailing on the Aegean Sea was a perfect way for her to unwind, to reflect, to lie in the sun, far from intrusive reporters and the pressures of her suddenly highly complicated life. "There's a difference between loneliness and solitude," she often said. Certainly, no screenplay could have offered a more glamorous or romantic setting for her to meet one of her hosts' friends. He wasn't tall; at five feet nine, he was Albert Finney's height. But he was a handsome, sensual, charming, accomplished young man, nine years Audrey's junior, from a respected and wealthy Italian family. He was a psychiatrist, and his specialty was the treatment of depression. With his sandy hair and outgoing manner, he was in some ways tantalizingly reminiscent of the young Bill Holden.

His name was Andrea Paolo Mario Dotti. Titles, like pasta, were plentiful in Naples, the city of his birth. At the age of fifteen he had seen *Roman Holiday*—and had fallen in love. "I'm going to marry that girl!" he told his mother. Now, face-to-face with her, he could hardly believe it. He told her they had met at a social gathering a few years back, but Audrey had no recollection of it. She certainly noticed him now, and he was even more impressed. She was delightful, bewitching, intelligent—and that smile! That laugh! Those eyes! The voice! The chemistry between them was undeniable, just as it had been with Holden and, more recently, with Finney. Audrey and Andrea, however, weren't making a movie. There was no dialogue to memorize, no shooting schedule to contend with.

His riveting dark eyes put him in clear command of the situation. An elemental electricity sparked their mutual desires. She was beginning to think that perhaps she wouldn't make any more movies. And instead of playing yet another character on-screen who was hopelessly in love, she would live the role—be that woman. Perhaps she could finally enjoy a sane domestic life, have a second child, and devote herself completely to raising her family.

Everything was happening so fast. Andrea's feelings for Audrey shone from his eyes. The princess, a sweet-natured woman, sang Andrea's praises. Audrey certainly wasn't depressed any longer; she looked very happy, always a vision in her seaworthy clothes, sometimes comfortable shiftlike dresses, often white slacks and pullovers in different colors, with her signature huge, dark-lensed sunglasses shielding her eyes from the bright Mediterranean sun. It seemed like a fantasy. Audrey and Andrea drank champagne from crystal glasses, the blue sky seeming to sparkle like the crystal. There were occasional forays into local villages along the route, an opportunity to dine ashore and shop. In the evenings they would hold hands and stroll along the gleaming mahogany deck of the vessel.

The shadow hovering over this fairy tale was the fact that Dr. Dotti was ecstatic to be entering into a relationship with *Audrey Hepburn*— film star extraordinaire, the perfect partner to accompany him everywhere, to proudly show off to the world. Of course they would have a family, and all that went with it, but nannies and servants would take care of all mundane domestic matters. Audrey could even make films, if she chose to (the offers never stopped coming). Dotti loved showing family and friends home movies he had taken of Audrey on their wondrous cruise. Even then, she'd been nervous about the camera angle and the lighting. Becoming a trophy wife, "arm candy," was never what Audrey had in mind, although she didn't know, in her ultra-vulnerable state, that that's what Andrea basically wanted. Would she have cared?

Even now, there was a sort of naïve innocence about her. He had swept her off her feet.

When Prince Aly Khan married Rita Hayworth, he had married the world's "Love Goddess," *Gilda* herself, and looked forward to Rita remaining exactly that. When he discovered that the real Rita was nothing like that image and was eager to abandon her film career and lead an out-of-the-spotlight private life, then as far as her prince was concerned, their marriage was finis. Of course, in Rita's case, during their courtship she had become pregnant, and the specter of scandal had made the prospect of marriage assume life-and-death proportions.

But that hadn't been the case with Grace Kelly. Her marriage, with all its drawbacks, was in its twelfth year. Rainier had remained adamant that she not resume her movie career, and Grace had been living a life and raising her three children without Hollywood dictating the terms, although a royal life in many ways dictated even stricter terms.

Perhaps Dr. Dotti would be the answer for Audrey. He seemed to understand her, describing her, years later, as someone who had to have matters under control and was afraid of surprises.

She phoned Givenchy, surprising him with her excitement on telling him that she was in love again. She talked with Capucine about the fears and doubts that are a part of every new romance. Doris Brynner was delighted for Audrey but cautioned her to take her time and not rush into anything. There were, after all, warning signs—Andrea had quite a temper—but romantic Audrey chose to ignore them.

Andrea may not have been a worldwide celebrity, but he wasn't exactly a nobody. He was a respected psychiatrist and neurologist, an assistant to the renowned Professor Leoncarlo Reda of Rome University. He was also a Catholic, as was Mel, and Audrey would soon be a divorced woman. She hadn't, however, married Mel in the Catholic Church. Still, the pope would have to issue a special dispensation.

Dotti's career might be threatened if he married an actress. His patients were supposedly from the highest echelons of Italian society, where show people were regarded as second-class citizens. Audrey, however, had a head start with this group. She was already friendly with, and very well liked by many of them. And, of course, she had a title herself.

It appeared that Dotti's family would be a problem—when Andrea got married, it was expected that he would produce heirs, many of them. To the family, Audrey was obviously beautiful, talented, and famous, but also close to middle age. Audrey faced yet another obstacle: Her mother didn't approve. The baroness hadn't liked Mel, either, and anyone could see how that had turned out. But Audrey's mind was made up.

On Christmas Eve 1968, Dotti asked Audrey to marry him. They were staying at their romantic weekend love nest, a friend's home on the island of Giglio, off the coast of Tuscany. He presented her with a huge, museum-quality diamond engagement ring from Bulgari.

Almost all obstacles had been overcome, including any issues with the Vatican. Dotti's mother, who was only in her mid-fifties and sometimes referred to Andrea as "Dr. Jekyll," had met and spent time with Audrey. She adored her. She found her shy, self-effacing, charming, and sincere. The rest of the Dotti family—his three brothers and their wives, his stepfather—were all equally charmed. They were surprised at her sense of humor, and all agreed that everything about her was appealing.

Winning over the Dottis had been an anxious undertaking; Audrey knew she would be under scrutiny and approached the situation with the same determination that characterized her film work. One might also assume she called on the same strength she had needed, years ago, on meeting Bill Holden's wife.

In the meantime, Audrey's divorce from Mel received as little attention in the press as possible. She had forgiven PR man Henry Rogers for questioning her relationship with Givenchy, they had remained friends, and he was representing her once again; this time his job was to keep her name out of the sensation-hungry media. Some of the older members of the international press corps were friends of Audrey's, having appeared with her in the press conference scenes in *Roman Holiday*. Audrey recognized the questionable qualities peculiar to European newsmen, and though she neither liked nor approved of them, she played the game.

Audrey and Andrea were married on January 18, 1969, only six weeks after her divorce from Mel became final, and four months before her fortieth birthday. She was now both a baroness and a countess.

Givenchy had created the perfect wedding ensemble for her—a pink, cowl-necked, short-skirted, long-sleeved dress, combining classic lines with an ultracontemporary look. The outfit would have been at home in the upscale scenes of *Two for the Road*. A face-framing foulard, a work of art in itself, fastened under the chin, was the finishing touch. She was a vision in pink, down to her stockings and shoes. She carried a small bouquet of flowers. Her makeup, in the same pastel hues as her dress, was flawless, and she looked twenty-five years old.

To avoid the voracious Roman paparazzi, they were married in the town hall of Morges, Switzerland, not too far from her beloved La Paisible. A crowd of onlookers clogged the streets, pushing and shoving for the best view. Obviously, the Swiss, under certain circumstances, were as celebrity conscious as anyone else.

Capucine, a bridesmaid, was smiling, but she didn't have much to be happy about. Turning forty couldn't have come at a worse time. Charlie Feldman had died a few months earlier, depriving her of his vital, generous friendship (he remembered her in his will). Whereas Audrey chose not to make films at this point, Cap had no choice, and the pickings were slim—the market for foreign films in America had dried up, and budgets were tight for films produced strictly for the European market. Audrey was deeply concerned about her friend's well-being.

At least Cap could count on Bill to help her financially. Holden, of course, was depressed that his Audrey was getting married again. He wasn't staying home obsessing about it, far from it, but he had recently completed Sam Peckinpah's *The Wild Bunch,* filmed in Mexico and Spain, and confided to co-star Warren Oates that he still considered Audrey the one great love of his life.

In 1971, Bill starred with Ryan O'Neal in the Blake Edwards film *The Wild Rovers.* Ryan and Bill became buddies, and on one occasion, the young actor asked him if he had ever fallen in love with one of his many beautiful leading ladies. "Yes, I did," replied Holden. "I fell in love with Audrey Hepburn." O'Neal was dazzled—that was the one *he* would have fallen in love with. O'Neal pressed on: did Audrey love him?

"I think so," replied Bill. "She wanted to get married. . . ."

∿•↽

To communicate his love of wildlife to the world, Bill had gone into partnership with producer David Wolper, who'd produced a recent film starring Holden, *The Devil's Brigade.* They planned to produce a nine-part television series on East Africa, to be narrated by Bill. Holden was determined to shatter the myth that Africa was a continent of jungle drums and tribal rituals, a myth largely created, in Bill's estimation, by Hollywood films.

The series would be called: *William Holden: Unconquered Worlds.* The scripts would be written by twenty-five-year-old David Seltzer. When they traveled to find locations for the series, Seltzer was not expecting Bill's sudden changes of personality after having a couple of drinks. The young writer contemplated resigning. Only one episode of the nine was produced: "Adventures at the Jade Sea," which was aired by CBS in March 1969.

At their wedding, Dotti and Audrey looked very happy; Paul Weiller was his best man, and his good friends Queen Frederika of Greece and Christina Ford, wife of Henry Ford II, were also on hand to support him. Audrey seemed uncomfortable at the intensity of the attention. Reporters asked if she and Dotti intended to have children. "Of course!" she replied, smiling broadly. She also said she intended to end her acting career to become "an Italian housewife." Her agents must have needed extra doses of Pepto-Bismol on hearing this pronouncement. But Audrey had worked from the age of thirteen, and for over twenty-five years straight. She felt she was ready for "a normal life."

In fact, she was making a huge adjustment. Few realized what it meant to be a member of that rare breed—"movie star." Stars were accustomed to attention night and day, from an army of devotees—hair and makeup people, publicists, designers, agents, writers, directors—and, in Audrey's as in many other cases, she'd had a manager-husband to "take care of things." All things. And to be a hatchet man when necessary. Suddenly all those elements were gone from Audrey's life—and they had provided a certain security and camaraderie that was comforting, pleasant, and distracting. Audrey had always been happy to listen to the troubles of those on her team, and to offer advice, and on occasion, help, when needed.

Now there was no team, only Dr. Dotti, their friends, and his family (her mother lived in San Francisco). Not that Audrey was without friends—one of her "dearest chums" was fashionista Arabella Ungaro, who had a beautiful home north of Rome in the choice district of Monti Pariloi. Signora Ungaro's residence was where Audrey would meet the occasional journalist for a rare interview. The Dotti domicile, and its location, for security reasons, was off-limits to the press.

Thank heaven Audrey's nine-year-old son liked Dotti, because he'd be living with his mother and new father, and attending the Lycée Chateaubriand in Rome. For Audrey, it was to be a life totally different from the one she'd led for the last decade and a half.

Within six months, she was pregnant. Physically, the next nine months would be very difficult. She would have to remain in bed much of the time.

Before she'd conceived, she led exactly the life that Andrea had been looking forward to. They moved from the Dotti family villa into a fabulous penthouse apartment overlooking the entire city. It was a thrilling vantage point from which to experience the beauty of Michelangelo's Roman dawn and sunset. At those moments, for Audrey it was as though Rome were a quiet, breathtaking movie set built only for her and Andrea. The couple went to parties, frequented nightclubs, attended special events, and even film premieres. The flashbulbs were blinding, but Dotti always welcomed the attention. Later reports claimed that, to Audrey's consternation, he would at times actually alert press and paparazzi to where he and his famous wife would be.

But Audrey looked happy; she seemed free at last, as though she had run away and joined the circus, exactly as she'd felt with Bill, before she married Mel. At Dotti's urging, she consented to a few interviews, in which she said how deeply in love she was. Did she have any interest in getting back on the screen? None—and when she said that

Mia Farrow, then twenty-three years old, could have her roles, she wasn't being facetious.

Regrettably, her happiness was short-lived. There were disturbing rumors that Andrea was being unfaithful—the Italian scandal magazines were worse than the old *Confidential*. She'd had to cope with rumors all her life, but she could hardly dismiss the gossip with an "Oh, Andrea!" And the stories always stressed the age difference between them.

She was in her seventh month, and it seemed the perfect time for her to return to La Paisible, her home in Tolochenaz, Switzerland, to prepare for the birth. Plenty of time for hysterics, and to read her husband the riot act, later. Being housebound would be difficult for someone who so enjoyed her social activities. But extra caution was essential. It was unlikely she would ever be able to bring another child to term, because of her physical condition after the many miscarriages. She was also facing the onset of menopause. She felt beholden to the Dottis, as well as to herself, Sean, and Andrea, of course, to deliver a healthy child.

∾•〰

It was hardly a secret—nightclubs and discos were Dr. Dotti's second home, its denizens his second family. He was a party animal, young and sexy, and so were the women prowling the territory. His stepson later described him as "a hound dog."

The Mod Generation was in full flower. There were no longer any rules. Propriety was an old-fashioned concept. Bill and Mel had been souls of discretion compared to Andrea, who loved to flirt and happily posed for photographs with the women eager to be seen with him. He was headline material now. He was Audrey Hepburn's husband. Audrey was mortified and angry. This educated and respected psychiatrist she had married, a man supposedly attuned to people's problems, was apparently too immature, too insensitive, to realize how he was hurting her.

Mel had been a strict overseer, with Audrey's welfare always of paramount concern. How she felt, what she wanted, her physical and mental well-being—they were what mattered most; it sometimes seemed that was all that had mattered. Dr. Dotti wanted his wife to be happy, but, on occasion, if she wasn't, why couldn't she work things out for herself? She wasn't a teenager but a sophisticated, resourceful, and intelligent woman. What was Audrey complaining about? At least Andrea, like many Italian men of means, didn't have more than one family—an official (that is, legal) one, consisting of wife and children whom he supported and saw on weekends; and an unofficial one, which he also supported, loved, and often lived with.

Mistresses and girlfriends were another story, a common part of the Italian male lifestyle. Audrey had to have known that when she married him. Wasn't that what had attracted her in the first place? Did she think she could change him? He loved her, she knew that; was that not enough? Clearly, Mel was not the only one with a double standard.

With Mel, it had been Marisol; now, with Dotti, it was Daniela (was the allure of women with a single name some sort of special aphrodisiac?). In Daniela's case, there was a punch line: according to many reports, Dotti was giving her psychiatric help. It was hardly a joking matter as far as Audrey was concerned. For the moment, all traces of her sense of humor seemed to vanish. "Poor Audrey" was not a label she was accustomed to. She had always been terrified of scandal, and her deep survival sense took hold. By remaining in Switzerland, she was able to insulate herself from the impact of all the ugly gossip, which she tried to ignore because she didn't want it to be true.

She concentrated on enjoying the peace and quiet, the invigorating climate and sheer beauty of her surroundings. Whether relaxing on a chaise longue, or tending to her immaculate gardens, or puttering around in the kitchen (friends gave five stars to her delicious salads), Audrey would postpone dealing with Andrea's behavior until the baby was born. Dotti, in true Italian fashion, was always smiling and attentive when he came to visit her in Switzerland, which he did often. This was his first marriage, and he was looking forward to becoming a first-time father.

On February 8, 1970, Audrey delivered, by cesarean section, a healthy baby boy. They named him Luca, in honor of one of Andrea's brothers.

Chapter

14

LATE IN 1971, CAPUCINE HAD SOME INTERESTING NEWS TO report about Bill. Her romance with him was over, but they had remained friends. She learned that he had finally divorced Ardis, after thirty years of marriage, and the about-to-be ex–Mrs. Holden would be receiving half of his $8-million fortune. Audrey wasn't surprised about the divorce—not after the vehicular manslaughter accident, and the death of Bill's younger brother and, in 1967, his father. What was surprising was that Ardis apparently blamed Bill's mother, Mary, who lived in an upscale retirement community not far from Bill's California home, for encouraging her son to take that final step.

Columns predicted that Pat Stauffer would be Holden's next wife, but Bill countered that he did not want to get married again. He commented that his divorce "cost me a small fortune . . . I had my independence, but the divorce was necessary to my way of thinking." And how was his relationship with Ardis, now they were divorced? "Marvelous."

She had nothing to say, then or later.

That year, Holden's good friend Marty Rackin, who'd been head of production at Paramount at the time of *Paris When It Sizzles*, offered him the starring role in *The Revengers*, a Western that Rackin hoped would follow in the successful footsteps of *The Wild Bunch*. Rackin suffered a heart attack while preparing the picture, and the studio wanted to replace him. Bill stood by his good friend: "No Rackin, no Holden." Bill prevailed.

Bill's co-star was another Rackin favorite, Susan Hayward (born Edythe Marrenner in Brooklyn, New York). A year older than Holden, she'd known Bill since they were both young contract players at Paramount. Since then both had scaled the heights and won Oscars. For Hayward, it had been a long, hard climb. "As an actor, Bill is generous," she noted. "He has enough ego that you respect him and he does his level best; and enough so he has room left over to care about the actor standing next to him."

One of those actors was Bill's twenty-six-year-old son Scott, who made his screen debut in a bit part as a cavalry lieutenant. Bill coached him, but he wasn't happy that Scott was pursuing what would be a short-lived career as an actor. The young man had received a degree in business administration, and businessman was a profession Holden thoroughly approved of.

It was a busy year for Bill. He was sober again, and he made the most of it. He starred in a film for Universal directed by Clint Eastwood. Eastwood had begun a hugely successful career as a director, and it was Jennings Lang who had signed him to the studio. *Breezy*, written by Eastwood's pal Jo Heims, was the story of a young hippie, played by up-coming young actress Kay Lenz, who has an affair with a conservative older man.

It was a venture dear to Eastwood's heart, the budget was low, and it had been conceived as a vehicle for Clint, who decided that Holden, at fifty-three, a dozen years older, would be better casting. Holden's salary wasn't $750,000-plus-a-percentage—not even close. In order to work with Eastwood, he agreed to do the role for nothing. *Breezy* wasn't expected to be a big moneymaker. Eastwood, candid as always, said up front that he did not expect it to make any money at all. It was a film he wanted to make because he loved Heims's script.

Scott Holden had a small role, playing a veterinarian. Production went smoothly. Discussing the finished product with Universal's New York publicity people, always an off-the-record, brainstorming-type get-together, Eastwood had only glowing things to say about Bill. He'd felt that he had delivered so many outstanding performances over the years that when they started shooting *Breezy*, Eastwood had been reluctant to give Bill any direction at all. But Bill told him early on not to hold back. "Every actor needs direction, Clint," he said.

Breezy was a positive experience for all concerned. As predicted, the film wasn't commercially successful. There was an amusing footnote: at a later point, Universal was contacted by the Screen Actors Guild. It was necessary that SAG member Holden be paid the scale salary of $4,000 for the six weeks he worked on the movie.

~•~

"It's wonderful, but I simply can't do it," Audrey told her agent, and turned down Sam Spiegel's offer to star in his epic production of *Nicholas and Alexandra*, based on the best-selling book by Robert K. Massie. Hepburn as the doomed czarina of Russia, in love with her husband, desperate about the poor health of their young son, enthralled by the spellbinding but evil Rasputin—this was indeed an enticing prospect and she would be perfectly cast. Location filming, however, would take her far away from home for a year, so it was out of the question: "I couldn't take the stress of being away from the children."

Warner Bros. offered her the starring role as the mother in *The Exorcist*, based on the best-selling novel by William Peter Blatty, a terrifying horror story based on the true story of a woman, a successful actress, whose young teenage daughter becomes possessed by a demon.

Audrey was now being offered mother-of-a-teenager roles? Playing a mother had been a bonanza for Joan Crawford, who was close to Audrey's current age when she made *Mildred Pierce,* and for Lana Turner, who was younger than Audrey was now when she made *Peyton Place* and *Imitation of Life.* On Warners' books, Audrey was box-office gold, with three huge winners: *The Nun's Story, My Fair Lady,* and *Wait Until Dark.* The director of *The Exorcist* would be William Friedkin, one of the best of the new breed. Her agents begged her to do it, and she agreed: if the picture were made in Rome. That ended that. The movie, which starred Ellen Burstyn, went on to become one of the biggest box-office hits of all time (*Nicholas and Alexandra* was far less successful). Audrey would have made millions—and perhaps would have won that second Oscar.

She didn't turn down all offers. She said yes to a request to appear in a TV special about the United Nations Children's Fund (UNICEF). It was fascinating to watch how the children were captivated by her, and it was obvious she returned the affection. The program was seen all over the world.

For a $1 million fee, she said yes to a TV commercial for a Japanese wig manufacturer. The commercial would air only in Japan, where Audrey was an icon. Other top stars, including Paul Newman and Steve McQueen, were doing commercials for Japanese companies, for the same $1 million fee. Filming took only four to five hours; $250,000 per hour wasn't bad for less than a day's work.

Dotti's family had obviously applied pressure on him to settle down and become a proper father and husband, and for the next several years the couple seemed to lead a traditional married life. Divorce was not an option for Audrey—she was going to be certain that Luca had the benefit of a mother *and* a father at home. Andrea's work fascinated her; his profession dealt with the workings of the mind. She wasn't a frivolous soul. She was a great fan of the films of Ingmar Bergman, whose dark excursions into the human psyche were hardly Neil Simon laugh riots.

Audrey felt complete—for a while. Baby Luca was a joy, and Sean was developing into a fine young man (by the age of fifteen, he would stand six feet three). She had stopped being an actress and had gotten her wish. She would become "an Italian housewife," an "ordinary" woman who would be home if her husband came home from work unexpectedly. Some Italian men expected that. She seemed content to go about her wifely, and motherly, chores, often unrecognized in the crowded streets of Rome. For the time being, one of the most famous women of the era was anonymous. She loved to shop in the many high-end Roman boutiques that had popped up; she didn't have the time or inclination anymore to spend endless hours being fitted for Givenchy couture. At home, there was a household staff, but Audrey was in charge. Then, once again, there were rumblings about her husband's wandering ways.

In Italy in the mid-1970s, there was political turmoil and life for the wealthy suddenly took on ominous, dangerous overtones. There was a rash of kidnap threats. A member of the prominent Bulgari family was successfully abducted. In Milan, potential victims were shot in the kneecaps. In Rome, when an attempt was made to kidnap Dotti, Audrey was terrified. It was all a chilling reminder of her World War II days. Bodyguards suddenly became essential employees; Audrey and Mel agreed that it was best for Sean, now fourteen, to be sent to a Swiss boarding school. Audrey and four-year-old Luca relocated to her beautiful Swiss home, where Dotti visited frequently. Her mother came to live with her for a while, supervising the domicile. But the baroness was growing older, and physical problems were taking their toll. Audrey wanted her close by, even though they didn't always get along. And she needed her for moral support—at the age of forty-five, she discovered she was pregnant again.

∽•↶

Audrey suffered another miscarriage that summer of 1974. In the midst of her sadness and depression, producer Ray Stark made her an offer to return to the screen. This time, encouraged by her husband, she expressed interest.

The vehicle appealed to her—it wasn't the typical sex-and-violence story that she abhorred. She'd turned down an opportunity, years earlier, to star in a Hitchcock film because of certain scenes in the script, especially one in which her character was being strangled. But sex, violence, and immorality summarized current film fare. Interestingly, Bill Holden shared Audrey's view of sex-on-screen: "In general, I don't care for scenes of copulation," he said. "Certain functions of the human body are private." He'd refused to do such a scene, back in 1969, for *The Christmas Tree,* a film directed by Audrey's great friend Terence Young. It took a visit to the Paris location from Pat Stauffer to convince Bill to cooperate, at least to an extent, as Young felt the scene essential to the story.

Audrey knew people associated her with a time when movies were pleasant, when women were beautifully dressed, and even the music was beautiful. Now, she felt, people were frightened by the movies. But she would always view herself as a realistic romantic—it was, she explained, possible to be both—and she still very much believed in love, a belief she shared with the character she was about to portray.

The original title of *Robin and Marian* had been *The Death of Robin Hood,* and the script was by James Goldman, who had written *The Lion in Winter.* Sean Connery would play Robin. When Audrey signed on, the title was changed to *Robin and Marian.* It was conceived to be a thoughtful, bittersweet, romantic tale, which had the unhappiest of endings—both Robin and Marian die, in a Romeo and Juliet–type plot turn. Only it's Marian who feeds Robin the poison, and then she drinks it herself, in what turned out to be an awkwardly staged scene.

Audrey was pleased that her role was age-appropriate. Although there were always offers to do so, at this point she would not play some version of Sabrina, the princess in *Roman Holiday,* or Holly Golightly. (Holden, on the other hand, resented the fact that he could no longer play the young leading man.)

Robin and Marian presented the lovers in troubled middle age. Marian had become a nun. It would not be a protracted shooting schedule—a mere six weeks, for which she'd be paid $1 million. The money would be welcome. Audrey's lifestyle, never extravagant like Elizabeth Taylor's (Taylor was "the last of the big splurgers," according to their mutual friend George Cukor), was nonetheless extremely costly. She was planning on buying more property in Switzerland, but she was wary, and nervous, at the prospect of facing the cameras again after such a long sabbatical. Her inner circle pointed out, and Audrey agreed, that in a worst-case scenario, where things didn't work out, it was hardly the end of the world.

She felt secure knowing that Richard Shepherd, who had co-produced *Breakfast at Tiffany's,* would be on board in the same capacity for *Robin and Marian.* Ray Stark had met all of her demands. Because shooting would take place in Spain, Audrey would take along Luca and his nanny, her makeup artist, her hairdresser, and an assistant.

A top supporting cast had been signed: Robert Shaw, Nicol Williamson, Denholm Elliott, and Kenneth Haigh. The major mistake was in selecting Richard Lester to direct. A top talent, he was none-theless the wrong choice. Lester's films were strictly fast-moving and action-packed—the Beatles' *A Hard Day's Night*, *A Funny Thing Happened on the Way to the Forum*, and *The Three Musketeers* were hardly tender love stories, although Connery was a big fan of Lester's work and wanted him on the film.

The problem wasn't that there was a generation gap between Hepburn and Lester. Audrey was only three years older. But she required, and was accustomed to, directors who knew how to present her—how to make her feel secure and loved. Wyler, Wilder, Donen, and the like were art-ists who had the patience, sensitivity, and desire to enable her to bloom into Audrey Hepburn, who, she was the first to admit, was a carefully wrought creation of actress, script, director, cameraman, costume de-signer, and all the craftsmen necessary to produce a great film.

She had no illusions about her abilities: "I'm no Laurence Olivier, no virtuoso talent." Some found it hard to believe, but it was true that she thought of herself as somewhat inhibited: "I find it difficult to do things in front of people." Reentering the moviemaking arena after eight years gave her stomachaches. Especially when it became clear, very early on, that she had made a wrong choice for her comeback. "Comeback" was a term she loathed: she'd never formally announced that she'd retired. How, therefore, could this be a comeback? Nonetheless, a key ad line promoting the film would be: "The Return of a Great Star."

Audrey had no rapport with Lester; no confidence in him. But she always gave every project her unconditional best, and this would be no exception. She soldiered on, even contending with a bout of dysentery along the way. She'd never made a movie with such a short shooting schedule and was unnerved that Lester was satisfied with one or two takes of a scene. With Wyler, she often repeated a scene dozens of times.

She shook with nerves before each take, and, in her polite but incisive way, let Lester know that sacrificing quality for speed was not the way she was used to working. If this was the current way of doing things, she had not been missing much.

She was forty-six, and angles, filters, and lighting were more important than ever. The cameraman was using a lot of natural light, which was unflattering to any actress over forty, especially one with an image to uphold. Audrey was very unhappy with the photography. On *Paris When It Sizzles* she had been able to have the cameraman replaced. That was not the case on *Robin and Marian*. No one seemed to care about such details.

In fact, Audrey looked good in the film, much better than she might have thought. The problems with the movie had nothing to do with her or her appearance. The first ten minutes, before she's even on-screen, were incredibly talky and boring. The renowned Richard Lester's talent-for-action scenes was glaringly absent. Attempts at humor were forced. In one of very few romantic moments, not many actresses could have played with such delicacy and strength the scene in which Marian tells Robin how handsome he'd been, what a wonderful body he had—"And it was all mine," she says wonderingly, her soft voice filled with exactly the right sentiment and emotion.

Critic Roger Ebert would astutely note: "What prevents the movie from really losing its way . . . are the performances of Sean Connery and Audrey Hepburn. . . . No matter what the director and writer may think, Connery and Hepburn seem to have arrived at a tacit understanding between themselves about their characters. They glow. They really do seem in love."

While in Spain, Audrey was disheartened and embarrassed when she saw photos of Dotti in the tabloids, posed in nightclubs with young women. "Don't believe what you see, believe what I tell you" was basically his explanation. Audrey later remarked: "Dotti was not much of an improvement over Ferrer." Actually, he was no improvement; at least Ferrer had been a partner in her career.

Ray Stark made certain *Robin and Marian* was launched in spectacular fashion. Although Connery was billed first, Audrey's name, beside his, was a line above it. The advertising slogan reflected the audience the producers were hoping to reach: "Love Is the Greatest Adventure of All." The film debuted at Radio City Music Hall in New York, and it was a major event. Columnist Earl Wilson later recalled: "It was one of those Ray Stark specials. I'd always found Audrey of interest, going back to her Bill Holden days. The lengths they'd gone to in order to cover that up! And now she was having big problems with the Italian doctor she'd married, and were doing their best to cover that up."

What made Audrey different, for Wilson, was the contrast between the women she'd played on-screen and the woman she was offscreen. The sex symbols could not get away with anything for long, "but the Hepburns could play a different game, unless they made a real blunder, like Ingrid Bergman. Today, of course, it doesn't matter. Look at Vanessa Redgrave!" Wilson had broken the big story, only a few years earlier, that the unmarried Redgrave was pregnant with her lover Franco Nero's child. Redgrave had casually revealed the fact to Wilson in the course of an interview and couldn't have cared less when the news broke. Wilson made certain that the publicist present at the interview would confirm the facts, if it became an issue.

There would never be any revelations from Audrey about her private life. Accompanied by Dotti, she had flown in to attend the Radio City opening. They'd momentarily resolved their differences. She was genuinely moved, and surprised, at audience reaction to her in-person appearance—she was truly idolized and loved (was it possible that it had been almost ten years since *Wait Until Dark* had premiered at this very theater?). She was terrified at the prospect of appearing onstage—there were more than 6,000 people in that audience—and backstage, her nerves almost got the best of her.

But if she'd had any doubts and concerns about the public having a short memory, and apparently she did, they disappeared after her reception. "We love you, Audrey," chanted many in the audience, and she was deeply moved.

Still, the $6-million movie turned out to be a big financial disappointment. At least Audrey was back on-screen, although she said she didn't know if she would ever make another film. Rumors were that there was another script she liked, but she wouldn't comment on it. It's unlikely she wanted *Robin and Marian* to be her swan song.

At this time, two women from Audrey's professional past—Edith Head, now in charge of costume supervision at Universal, and Sheilah Graham, still writing a syndicated gossip column—were brought together for an interview, in the Edwardian Room of the Plaza Hotel, to publicize Head's affiliation with Universal. They were both dressed in black. It was late afternoon, the room was almost empty, and the two women couldn't decide where to sit, changing tables and chattering all the while. Finally, to the relief of the nervous maître d', a table was chosen.

The gossip was nonstop, and at one point the young Universal publicist who had set up the meeting mentioned that it was wonderful, wasn't it, that Audrey Hepburn was back on the screen? There was dead silence from both women. "Just wonderful!" snapped Head, with Graham telling the publicist: "You're too young, dear, to know what Edith has been through with Audrey. But you're right, she's still a big star." Graham turned to Head: "—and so are you, Edith!"

Chapter

15

R E-TEAM AUDREY, BILL, AND BILLY WILDER?
Jennings Lang was a big fan of Wilder's. He had signed the
director, now in his seventies, to a deal with Universal. The first film
had been Wilder's disappointing remake of *The Front Page,* and when
Wilder came to New York to promote it, Audrey's name came up. At
a luncheon for the foreign press, he was asked by reporters whether he
would be working with her again. "Everyone still wants to work with
her, including me," he replied. "She's the one who doesn't want to work.
Being a mommy is her current career!"

Tom Tryon had written a best-selling novel about Hollywood,
Crowned Heads, and one of its stories, "Fedora," was slated to become
Wilder's next Universal film. It wasn't, as columnists joked, the story
of a hat. The title was the name of a mysterious, Garbo-like actress,
and the plot had overtones of *Sunset Boulevard* and other films about
Hollywood, with a bizarre mother-daughter twist.

Bill Holden would be playing the male lead. He was hot again, and
when casting suggestions were tossed around for the title role, absurd
as it may have seemed, Audrey's name came up. Hepburn's persona was
not remotely Garbo-like, but then again, when the studio produced
Gable and Lombard in 1976, their initial choice for the role of the shimmering, blonde, legendary Carole Lombard was the black-haired, absolutely nothing-like-Lombard, quintessential rock-and-roller Cher (Jill

Clayburgh got the part).

The resurgence of interest in Bill Holden was not the result of any great drive on his part to recapture his former glory. He simply wanted to work, and he had scored several successes—on television, in the police drama *The Blue Knight;* on the big screen in *The Towering Inferno,* which he loathed. He'd had to take third billing and resented the attention, and the screen time, lavished on top-billed Paul Newman and Steve McQueen. Not to mention that Jennifer Jones, with whom Bill had scored a tremendous success two decades earlier in *Love Is a Many Splendored Thing*—was relegated to below-the-title status. Faye Dunaway had the female star part.

But Bill was happy to be in a blockbuster, and they'd met his price of $750,000. It had been a long time. He had scored a major critical triumph, along with Faye Dunaway, in the highly acclaimed Paddy Chayevsky–Sidney Lumet film *Network.* With nonalcoholic vigor, Holden memorably portrayed an angry, aging television executive, and the performance won him an Oscar nomination as Best Actor. Top-billed Dunaway won the Oscar for Best Actress, and Peter Finch, posthumously, for Best Actor. Holden and Finch, also a heavy drinker, had become good friends, as had Holden and Chayevsky.

Director Lumet had cast Holden because of "the look of sadness on his face." Dunaway later said he had brought "a crusty elegance" to the role, "a perfect combination of street smarts and schooled intellect."

Bill had built himself a beautiful home in Palm Springs, sitting on two-and-a-half acres, in the gated Southridge community. It was an 8,000-square-foot desert retreat with wonderful views, high ceilings, and floor-to-ceiling windows. The master bedroom suite boasted two fireplaces, a walk-in closet thirty-six feet long, a sunken terrazzo spa tub, and an indoor-outdoor shower. The house had four bedrooms, four-plus baths, a guest suite, a wood-paneled media room, and a gym. An infinity pool was cantilevered over boulders. The estate rivaled Sinatra's Palm Springs compound, and Bill could never complain that he wasn't living well.

His personal life seemed to have settled into something stable and satisfying. He'd been sober for three years. Pat Stauffer had remained an important presence in his life, and he would even deliver the eulogy at her father's funeral. But All-American Bill seemed to conduct his private life in very European-like fashion, not unlike Mel Ferrer and Andrea Dotti. He met and fell in love with actress Stefanie Powers, née Stefanie Zofya Paul, a beautiful young brunette with an adventurous spirit. To experience again the first blush of true love was a feeling Bill was not about to deny himself. When they met, Powers was at a low ebb emotionally, having just divorced her husband, actor Gary Lockwood. Bill understood. He was an old-school gentleman, with his great charm intact, and she credited him with making her "feel like a human being again."

For Bill, with Stefanie, there was a different dynamic in play. "Most of my life I've had to take care of people," he said, "but when I'm with Stef, I haven't had to do anything." In fact, she protected him. She appreciated his self-deprecating humor and sense of fun; Bill still drove a motorcycle, and she was often a backseat passenger.

"We were soul mates," she said. They came into each other's lives at exactly the right moment. "I've never had a relationship so fulfilling," he said. If Audrey heard about those comments, she was long past taking them personally; hadn't he said similar things about her and Grace Kelly more than twenty-five years earlier? But Capucine and Pat Stauffer's feelings must have been hurt on hearing Bill express those sentiments.

Powers, at thirty-two, was twenty-four years Holden's junior. There was a physical resemblance to the younger Audrey, and like Audrey, Stefanie was devoted to her mother. She was an outdoors girl, and she loved to travel; the serenity and allure of exotic locales appealed to her. But on her travels with Bill, the couple didn't spend time seeking out wonderful restaurants. They preferred to explore the territories they visited, and to understand their people and customs.

Bill introduced Stefanie to his great passion: Africa, and wildlife preservation. "Bill was an environmentalist before the word had been invented," she noted, pointing out: "He was a very interesting man. There was much more to him than the fact that he was 'a big movie star.'" Virtually no woman in Bill's life ever complained that one of his shortcomings was being impressed with who he was. Perhaps he would have been better off if he had been impressed with who he was, and with what he had accomplished. Not appreciating the quality of his work was a trait he shared with Audrey—the irony was how hard they'd both worked to create their performances.

The young male stars of the 1970s were not strangers to Holden's films. Jack Nicholson, visiting a friend one afternoon at Cedars of Lebanon Hospital in Hollywood, spotted a Mercedes in the parking lot. It was the exact model he was planning to buy. He walked over for a closer look—a man was trying to locate something in the back seat. Nicholson tapped on the window. The two men immediately recognized one another, exchanging a friendly, "Oh, hi!" It turned out that Holden was a longtime idol of Nicholson's. He asked Bill how he liked the car, which the older actor recommended enthusiastically. "I've tried them all," said Bill, "Rolls-Royce, Bentley, Jaguar." Nicholson asked Holden why he was at Cedars. "Oh, I'm going in for a two-day drying out period," he replied, locating at last the six-pack of beer he'd been searching for in the backseat. "Come up to my room and we'll talk," said Bill, and they did, for quite a long time. The men rarely encountered one another afterward, but when they did they felt like "old friends."

John Belushi was a big Holden fan. They encountered each other at the well-known La Costa Resort, located just north of San Diego in Carlsbad, California. Bill and Belushi were there for the same purpose—to dry out.

Bill, almost thirty years Belushi's senior, was the voice of experience when he warned the younger star, whose film, *Animal House,* was proving to be a big hit but whose problems with substance abuse had made headlines, to expect the press to keep him in their sights. "They'll be good to you when you're on top," he told Belushi. "But if you start to slip a little, they'll try to tear you down."

∽•∾

Bill and Stefanie maintained separate homes, and he was not uncomfortable referring to Powers as the woman he lived with. "Marriage? Why spoil things?" he said. Stefanie was a positive influence on him, and he was grateful. Later, when he did propose marriage, she turned him down. He was drinking again, and the unpredictable, irrational behavior had returned. Rumor had it that he'd held a gun to his head for an hour and a half when she told him she wouldn't marry him.

When reporter Bernard Drew bluntly asked Holden, "Why all the drinking?" Holden replied: "Let's just say inner turmoil." When drunk, Bill's behavior was so erratic that when the Reagans occupied the White House, the first couple of the land thought it best not to invite their old friend to any official functions. It was anyone's guess what he might do after he'd had one too many, and he knew it. For that reason, he turned down an invitation to Reagan's inauguration.

At one point, Bill owned a pet snake, "Bertie," that sometimes coiled itself around him; on one occasion, when Bertie couldn't be found, Bill's houseguests, Helen and Marty Rackin, said they'd have to leave if Bertie wasn't located (he was). "Yes, Bill could be eccentric, but he was always a likable, persuasive, intelligent guy," noted his pal, actor Cliff Robertson. "The lions and tigers couldn't have had a better advocate."

◡•◡

What became of the possibility of re-teaming Hepburn, Holden, and Wilder? Audrey would have been very expensive; and, remembering the fiasco of *Paris When It Sizzles,* it was highly unlikely she would have the remotest interest in working with Bill ever again, although Billy Wilder would have been welcome.

How about Elizabeth Taylor for the part? Neither Bill nor Billy had ever worked with Elizabeth. "Have you seen her lately?" was Jennings Lang's reply (Taylor was forty-six; she'd put on weight, loved her martinis, and had become difficult to photograph—no close-ups until after lunch, when the puffiness in her face had subsided). Finally, a rising young foreign star, Marthe Keller, was cast. "Who?" asked Universal PR executive Paul Kamey, on learning of the choice; it was a reaction subsequently echoed by the American public, and a move Wilder deeply regretted. In the meantime, Universal withdrew from the project, and Wilder subsequently had a tough time securing financing and distribution. Holden had already slashed his salary so that Billy could get the picture made.

Back when Wilder had been in New York promoting *Front Page,* Audrey was on his mind. During lunch with a reporter at the Laurent Restaurant, he was asked if he planned on getting together with Gloria Swanson, who had an apartment in New York. Their classic *Sunset Boulevard,* with Bill Holden, was constantly shown on television, at film festivals, and in revival houses. It already had a huge cult following.

186

Wilder said he'd try to see her, and noted, with a tinge of disbelief: "Do you realize that Audrey Hepburn today is close to the age Swanson was when she made *Sunset Boulevard*?"

Swanson had been forty-nine when she made the classic film. Audrey was soon to turn fifty.

~·~

He was urban, American, New York–gritty. And he was dark and sexy, very much Audrey's type. The son of Italian immigrants (his parents were of Sicilian origin), Biagio Anthony Gazzarra—Ben Gazzara—said that discovering acting in his teen years growing up in the Kips Bay section of Manhattan rescued him from what might have been a life of crime. He attended City College of New York for two years, then dropped out to study acting, first with director Erwin Piscator at the New School, then the Actors Studio. Rex Reed later described him as "the Actors Studio crown prince" and made the point that in his characterizations, Gazzara "never hid behind mumbles and scratches," as did many other Studio alumni.

Audrey was impressed that Ben had achieved success on the Broadway stage. He won wide acclaim for *A Hatful of Rain*, and he had created the role of Brick in *Cat on a Hot Tin Roof*. Later in life, Gazzara said he turned down many film offers in those early days. "I won't tell you the pictures I turned down because you'll say, 'You are a fool,' and I was a fool." A sense of humor did reside in the seemingly ultraserious Gazzara. It surfaced during appearances he made on TV talk shows. And, like Mel, he had even appeared as a panelist on *What's My Line?* A successful weekly TV drama series, *Run for Your Life*, brought him widespread recognition.

He was delighted to be Audrey's leading man in *Bloodline;* he was not usually cast as a romantic lead. The film was based on Sidney Sheldon's best-selling novel (in ads for the movie, the title would be explained: "The line between love and death is the Bloodline"). A crisis in Audrey's personal life led her to accept the role.

By April 1978, her marriage to Dotti had run its course. The divorce became final three years later, and Dotti didn't make it easy. The fact that he'd entertained his girlfriends in their apartment was the final straw. Incredibly, she blamed herself for the breakup of this marriage, a union she'd poured her heart and soul into. Her unconditional love hadn't been enough. With this failure, she once again lost the concept of creating a family, which was the prime aim of her existence.

Now she had two children by two fathers, and two divorces. In that respect, she was no better than her mother, and she felt her sons were emotionally reliving her childhood. Audrey's friends were deeply concerned about her emotional state in this time.

Bloodline was a lifeline. Escaping back into her career would, she hoped, enable her to survive this latest blow. The film she had really wanted to do a couple of years earlier was *The Turning Point,* a story of the ballet world, with a tour-de-force role as a legendary prima ballerina on the verge of forced retirement. She had asked for the part, but Anne Bancroft had already been cast. Hepburn would always refer to this film as "the one that got away"—and it also got away from Audrey's former fellow Dream Girl, Princess Grace. Grace, on the board of directors of 20th Century-Fox, had been given a copy of the Arthur Laurents script. She loved it and sent it on to Prince Rainier for approval. A comeback at last! But permission was, once again, denied.

The *Bloodline* script was rambling. Sheldon's novel was a fun read (he had a huge female readership), but it didn't translate into a good script. Audrey would at least be comfortable with the director, her old pal Terence Young. A $1-million-plus salary closed the deal. She'd be playing the glamorous heiress to a pharmaceutical fortune (in the book, the character was in her early twenties). Gazzara would be the firm's CEO, and they marry after her father, the owner of the firm, dies in a questionable accident.

There was—or was supposed to be—spellbinding intrigue, mystery, and danger. Filming would take place on international locations, with an all-star supporting cast, including James Mason, Irene Papas, Maurice Ronet, Romy Schneider, Beatrice Straight, Gert Fröbe, and Omar Sharif. None of them were happy with the script or their roles. Apparently, all had done it for the money.

Audrey arrived on location accompanied by a bodyguard. Personal security had become a prime concern. To some, it appeared she'd had a face-lift, and a new hairstyle gave her a different look. For the first time on-screen, she would be smoking a lot of cigarettes (always gracefully, of course). Offscreen, she still chain-smoked.

~•~

With Gazzara, Audrey was once again repeating the Holden scenario, with a major difference: this time she was calling the shots. She made the first move, and it was not subtle. Her gently aggressive character in *Charade* might have done exactly the same thing to capture the reluctant Cary Grant's attention.

Gazzara, seated in his canvas chair one morning on the set, was waiting to be called. He was reading a book. Audrey walked over to him. He looked up from his book and told her he had begun it last night and couldn't sleep. She replied that she had the same problem: "When it happens to you again, feel free to call me. We'll keep each other company." They soon discovered they had more in common than insomnia. They were nearly the same age (Gazzara was a year younger). Ben's second marriage, to actress Janice Rule, was, like Audrey's, on the rocks. As was the case with Audrey and Mel, it was Gazzara's career, not Rule's, that had skyrocketed. Janice Rule was beautiful and talented, but the camera didn't love her. Kim Novak ended up landing the role in the movie version of *Picnic*, which Rule had created on the stage.

"Audrey was unhappy in her marriage and hurting; I was unhappy in my marriage and hurting, and we came together and we gave solace to each other and we fell in love," recalled Gazzara. When they discussed their marital woes, she was candid about the Dotti mess; she even confided that at one point she'd considered suicide—certainly only a fleeting feeling, one she would never have contemplated seriously, not with her two boys to consider.

As with Bill, the chemistry was there from the start. After filming a love scene, Gazzara knew for certain that she wasn't acting. After they got to know each other, he was shocked to discover how unsure she was of her talent. "We were having a drink in Munich . . . and she told me, 'Do you know, Ben, I never thought I was a good actress.'" He found her "so self-effacing, and that's why, on the screen, she was so genuine because what you saw on the screen you saw in life—that smile and the way she lit up a room She just had it."

Still—a Tony for *Ondine*, an Oscar for *Roman Holiday*, five other Oscar nominations, including one for her inspired work in *The Nun's Story*, the impact she'd had in *Breakfast at Tiffany's*, eight Golden Globe nominations. After all she had accomplished, the stardom she had achieved and sustained, she still had doubts about her acting ability?

She considered herself strictly the product of great directors. Perhaps the success itself had come too easily—she'd certainly put in the hard work, and then some, to achieve the performances. She was still putting in the hard work, and Gazzara said he spent a great deal of their time together trying to convince Audrey that she was a great actress.

At the beginning of the affair, the couple agreed that their relationship would be an interlude that would last only as long as the making of *Bloodline*. Audrey, too much of a romantic at heart, soon felt herself wanting this to be more.

When filming on *Bloodline* wrapped early in 1979, so did their affair. Or so he thought. "Audrey had a life in Europe and Switzerland," he said; his home bases were Los Angeles and New York. "It was impossible. Life got in the way of our romance." But unlike her affairs with Bill and Albie, what transpired between Audrey and Ben would find its way into a script.

Meanwhile, Terence Young's next film, to be made in Korea, was to star Gazzara, and Audrey was pleased that her son Sean would be a production assistant. Although both Rome and Tolochenaz, Switzerland, were far from Korea, she'd have a legitimate reason to drop in on the set.

However, Gazzara would soon be involved with the woman who would soon become the next Mrs. Gazzara. When the Gazzaras subsequently traveled to Rome, Audrey, according to Ben, contacted him at his hotel. She wanted to see him. He replied that that would not be possible, then called her back to explain. He recalled that when she answered the phone, he remained silent—neither of them said anything. She didn't say his name, but finally, "She simply whispered, 'Good-bye.'"

He later said, "I was flattered that someone like that would be in love with me. . . ." Gazzara also said that Audrey had told others that he'd broken her heart. "She was so kind and sweet," he said. "And I hurt her."

But it wasn't good-bye; far from it.

In true Hollywood fashion, there was a project that would bring them back together. It was conceived by Gazzara's buddy, director Peter Bogdanovich, one of the premier directors of the 1970s. His films had their roots firmly embedded in those of the great directors of the 1930s and 1940s. Recently, there had been expensive Bogdanovich bombs, including *At Long Last Love* and *Nickelodeon*. This new project, *They All Laughed,* was in part inspired, if that's the word, by Gazzara's romance with Audrey. The two men collaborated on the script, which was credited to Bogdanovich and Blaine Novak, with the hope that she would play the part.

Was there any chance that Hepburn would play a character in any way based on herself? Well, she very well might. She still had feelings for Gazzara. What better way to rekindle their relationship? They would live it all out on-screen, and magically all the hurt between them might disappear. The film would be shot entirely in New York, and Sean, now nineteen, was going to be hired as a production assistant (and would play a small role in the film).

Dotti was continuing to present problems, and the animosity between husband and soon-to-be ex-wife was affecting their relationship with their son Luca. For Audrey, escaping to New York, and the insulated world of filmmaking, was a welcome prospect.

Audrey's signing on would enable Bogdanovich to secure financing (in addition to the millions of his own money he was investing in the production). The shooting schedule, like that for *Robin and Marian*, was only six weeks, and Audrey would be paid her usual $1 million. It's a moot point whether she was aware that Bogdanovich was planning on *They All Laughed* to be the launching pad for his new star discovery, twenty-year-old Dorothy Stratten. At one point Bogdanovich considered casting himself in the role of the man who falls in love with Stratten, but the part eventually went to John Ritter.

From a professional point of view, Audrey might have been concerned, if "presenting" Ms. Stratten, as Audrey had been presented in *Roman Holiday, Sabrina,* and so on, was the director's intention and preoccupation. Where would that leave her? Stratten was a beautiful blonde, reminiscent of a very young Cybill Shepherd (another Bogdanovich discovery, ten years Stratten's senior). Stratten had been a *Playboy* centerfold, and a Playmate of the Year. She had virtually no acting experience, but she did have a fiercely possessive, violent husband, who was jealous of her impending big break and Bogdanovich's interest in her. Audrey had something in common with Ms. Stratten: both were of Dutch descent.

Bloodline opened in June 1979, to mostly poor reviews. In New York City, at the Tower East Theater on Manhattan's East Side, there were lines around the block. Elsewhere, at theaters throughout the city, the country, and the world, there were lots of empty seats. Audrey and Ben did not look particularly good together on-screen. The couple's chemistry offscreen didn't ignite any sparks on-camera. Box-office rentals for the film fell considerably below its cost. Audrey had made a dud.

Romantic comedy à la *They All Laughed,* conceived partially as an update of the classic French film *La Ronde,* suited Gazzara about as well as it would have the late Edward G. Robinson. When, before production began, it became obvious that Gazzara was no longer interested in Audrey romantically, an icy calm took hold of her. She wasn't beyond anger, and she responded in the way anyone in a similar position would, if they could: she decided to walk out on the film. If the financing that her name guaranteed took a walk, too, that would be Bogdanovich's—and Ben's—problem to work out. Her sensibilities had been abused and she had been hurt.

Just as it all began to feel overwhelming—this terrible mess of a life one could get into by the age of fifty—she made a telephone call to someone she had met a while ago on the West Coast. She had a warm feeling that something good might result. But she wasn't placing any bets on it.

Chapter

16

H ERE WAS A MAN WHO, WITH THE EXCEPTION OF BILL HOLDEN all those years ago, seemed to understand, at once, the difference between what Audrey did for a living—what she was famous for—and who she really was. They were not the same thing.

Back in 1966, when Audrey's *How to Steal a Million* was in release, and *Two for the Road* was in production, Dutch-born actor Robert Wolders got an important break when he was cast in *Laredo*, the hit TV series set in the Old West. "My character was supposed to be a combination of Errol Flynn, 007, and Casanova!" he later recalled, and found it amusing that though he'd never ridden a horse or held a gun, those were the essentials for his role as Ranger Erik Hunter. There were numerous changes of Western garb for every episode, which led him to feel as though he looked like he'd be leading a Gay Pride parade. "I had to wear those costumes, I was under contract," he said. But his female co-stars in the episodes, and other colleagues, knew without a doubt "that I was straight."

In 1975, when Audrey was filming *Robin and Marian* in Spain, Wolders, with much fanfare, had appeared on American television's top-rated *The Mary Tyler Moore Show* in an episode entitled, "Not Just Another Pretty Face." He was the "pretty face," a very continental, handsome, sexy man Mary is dating with whom she has nothing in common, so she becomes concerned that their relationship is superficial. There had been a lot of interest in Wolders playing the role, because he'd been very much in the entertainment news. He had just married a film star from Hollywood's Golden Era, Merle Oberon, who, at sixty-four, was twenty-five years his senior. Wolders had played Oberon's love interest a couple of years earlier in her self-produced comeback vehicle, *Interval*. They fell in love and she divorced her South American millionaire husband (who was enraged by the turn of events) to marry Wolders.

Exotic glamour had always been Oberon's trademark. She'd even risen to the rank of aristocrat, as Lady Korda, during her marriage to British film mogul Sir Alexander Korda. But, in fact, from the beginning of her career, she had done a masterful job of inventing herself: the former Estelle Merle O'Brien "Queenie" Thompson, at one time a dance-hall hostess, was strictly cinema royalty. Born the daughter of an Indian nurse's assistant and an Irish mechanical engineer, she proved to be a talented actress with at least three classic films to her credit: Korda's *The Private Life of Henry VIII*, *The Scarlet Pimpernel*, and William Wyler's *Wuthering Heights*.

The public would have been surprised to learn, as Wolders undoubtedly was, that there was another side to Oberon. She had two adopted children whom she adored. There was an element of whimsy in her that ran counter to her cinematic image as a remote beauty. Roddy McDowall was a close friend of the actress, and on one occasion he took home movies of her when she, along with Natalie Wood, George Cukor, and others, visited his beach house for one of his informal afternoon gatherings. Oberon came in strictly casual attire: slacks and a blouse, no jewelry, her jet black, waist-length hair fashioned into a flowing ponytail. She appeared to be having a very good time.

Audrey and Merle Oberon had been acquaintances for years. Back in 1976, they'd posed together—quite a contrast in generations—with

William Wyler, who looked more or less the same as he always had, at the American Film Institute's tribute to the director.

Hepburn was certainly aware of Wolders once he became Merle's husband. Oberon suffered from a serious heart ailment and had required open-heart surgery—not yet the routine operation it would become in ensuing decades. She prided herself on her beautiful skin, and the surgery had left her with a terrible scar down the middle of her chest. During her recovery, Wolders cared for her night and day, much as Mel had cared for Audrey after she broke her back during production of *The Unforgiven*. But Merle's health declined rapidly, and she died in 1979. They'd been married only four years, and reports were that she left him a fortune (at auction, her jewels fetched over $2 million).

A year earlier, Audrey and Wolders—"Rob"—had been seated alongside each other at a dinner party at the beautiful Beverly Hills home of their mutual friend Connie Wald. The former Constance Emily Polan was a leading West Coast hostess, widow of Brooklyn-born producer Jerry Wald, the man who was the prototype for Budd Schulberg's classic Hollywood novel of the ultimate showbiz scoundrel, *What Makes Sammy Run?* Before his sudden death from a heart attack at the age of fifty, Wald had produced many renowned films, including *Mildred Pierce, Johnny Belinda,* and *An Affair to Remember,* as well as Marilyn Monroe's penultimate film, *Let's Make Love.* Wald and Connie were major players on the Hollywood scene.

Connie was Audrey's closest California-based friend, and she'd been Audrey's houseguest in Switzerland on many occasions. Like Audrey, Connie had two sons, and fashion was another of the two women's mutual interests. Both took great pride in their homes, with informality the keynote when they entertained. If Audrey was Connie's overnight guest, it wasn't unusual for them to quibble over who would do the dishes.

Rob and Audrey, comfortable and at ease enjoying Connie's hospitality, had plenty to commiserate about. Audrey's pending divorce loomed large, and Rob had recently lost Merle. He was five feet ten, with compassionate green eyes and an agreeable disposition; he was not the aggressive, domineering type. Although lightning didn't strike à la Holden—nor, as she was later to say, was it Romeo and Juliet—they certainly hit it off. He became "Robbie" to her, Rob to her friends. They had more than a great deal in common, not the least of which was their shared Dutch heritage, and she loved hearing him speak the language. But the time was hardly right for either to pursue a relationship.

The troublesome *They All Laughed* was occupying all her time and thoughts—she was prepared to abandon the film, and damn the professional consequences. She'd been putting on a great front. The media were excited to have her back in Manhattan, and she played along. Why not, for a change? She was seen in the right restaurants, shopped at Bergdorf's, went to an occasional Broadway show, and so forth. But she was almost always with female companions, careful to exercise discretion. She didn't want to provide Dotti with any ammunition in their divorce proceedings. She was chagrined when there were column items linking her romantically with director Bogdanovich.

There were still a few movie-fan magazines in existence, and Audrey was quoted in one of them: "Aging doesn't bother me—loneliness does." When she telephoned Rob in Los Angeles, he recognized the call as a cry for help. Immediately, he flew to New York, where Audrey was living at the Pierre Hotel on Fifth Avenue, a favorite hostelry for Europe's well-heeled (the studio was footing the bill). The time was right, and Rob and Audrey shared a mutual respect. She was happy being with him; he was fun and intelligent. He relieved her anxieties. He was patient and understanding, and her sense of humor began to return. She'd found someone she could relax and laugh with, tell anything to. Rob was quick to sense anything that displeased her.

"I saw them together, in the lobby of the Pierre, waiting for the elevator," recalled Pat Gaston Manville. "They weren't holding hands, but their hands were touching, and they seemed so at ease and comfortable with each other. She was glowing. I remember I had encountered Audrey with Mel in Europe, years earlier, around the time she'd made that film with Gary Cooper, and I didn't observe the kind of warmth between them that Audrey seemed to have with this new man in her life."

Because Audrey was under the scrutiny of Dotti's lawyers, the couple could not be seen together in public. They decided that Rob would move to Europe and live in Switzerland.

Meanwhile, fulfilling her commitment to star in *They All Laughed* suddenly seemed a far less disagreeable prospect, not to mention having to deal with a potential breach-of-contract suit. Her son was happy to have been hired to work on the film. She didn't want to disappoint him. And a commitment was a commitment. Professionalism was one of Audrey's greatest assets.

Now, however, neither Audrey nor Ben had any romantic interest in the other. Gazzara had no idea Rob had entered Audrey's life. When there had been an attraction between them, the on-screen results, in *Bloodline,* had been negligible. What would be in store for their love story on-screen in *They All Laughed?*

As in *Breakfast at Tiffany's,* the action in *They All Laughed* would take place all over town. New York City would be a supporting player in the story. Audrey's look in the film was intact, perfectly balanced and detailed, whether she disembarked from a helicopter or strolled down New York's streets in pencil-thin jeans, designer boots, and trademark oversized sunglasses. Her hairdo, though—what seemed like piles of curls atop her head—wasn't flattering.

It was evident early on that Bogdanovich's vision for the picture didn't seem to be translating memorably onto celluloid. The pace was tortoise-like, and Hepburn and Gazzara were even more mismatched than in *Bloodline*. At least in that film there had been an attempt to make Gazzara look polished and urbane.

In one scene, in bed together after making love, they are speaking intimately, facing each other, the camera very close. It was the kind of lingering shot Hitchcock might have used when working with Cary Grant and Grace Kelly, or with Grant and Ingrid Bergman; the kind of shot Billy Wilder might have used for Hepburn and Holden. In the make-believe world of on-screen romance, the effect of such scenes relies on the charisma of the actors, and their physical attractiveness. Whereas Audrey's face was made for the camera, her leading man's, at this stage, wasn't. Their characters did not come across as a romantic couple.

But surely Bogdanovich knew what he was doing. After all, three of his films—*The Last Picture Show, What's Up, Doc?* and *Paper Moon*—were 1970s classics. But, as Garson Kanin once said, "Good direction can make a good script better, but there's nothing in the world the director can do to make a bad script good." Even, apparently, if the director is coauthor of the script.

According to reports, the disruptive presence of Dorothy Stratten's husband in her life hovered menacingly over *They All Laughed*, even when the cameras weren't rolling. She was being urged by those expecting her to become a major star (among them *Playboy's* Hugh Hefner) to seek a friendly divorce and make it financially worthwhile for him. In the meantime, Stratten was in awe of Hepburn's talent and professionalism, and she didn't miss an opportunity to watch her work.

Production continued from April through July 1980. It may have been the most dismal professional experience Audrey had ever had. At least on *Robin and Marian,* she'd had Sean Connery to work with. No one was more aware than Audrey that it was almost impossible to predict the final result. The writing of the *Sabrina* script, day by day, had taught her that. But no one with an objective eye could have been chortling happily at the prospects for *They All Laughed.*

On August 14, after production had wrapped, a real-life turn of events occurred, one that went beyond any screenwriter or director's imaginings, although those close to the situation wouldn't have ruled it out. Beautiful Dorothy Stratten, not even twenty-one, was brutally murdered by her husband, who then killed himself. Not since the murder of Sharon Tate and her friends in 1969 had such a tragedy shaken the film community.

A year later, *They All Laughed* was released. Finding a distributor had been a problem: "You can smell a bomb when you see one," noted Bob Wilkinson, Universal's New York–based vice president of sales. The film, unfortunately, was boring, despite Sinatra's exciting rendition on the soundtrack of the classic Cole Porter song. One major critic opined that Audrey on-screen had been treated "shabbily" by the director, not to mention what a wasted opportunity it had been for both actress and director. It was noted that Gazzara seemed a frozen, humorless presence and couldn't even smile convincingly. The film ended up earning less at the box office than the reported $1 million Audrey had been paid to make the movie.

As usual, in later years, certain cultists embraced it. One is reminded of Cukor's evaluation of his own dismal *Two-Faced Woman,* and of his opinion of another of his flops, *Sylvia Scarlett,* which had starred then-at-her-peak Katharine Hepburn and Cary Grant: "I'd use it as an insanity test," Cukor said. "When people said to me . . . 'Oh, I loved that picture!' I used to tell them, 'Now I know about you, your mind is not too good.'"

They All Laughed was such a financial debacle that for many of the hotshot directors of the 1970s, it brought to an end to studio acquiescence to their demand for final cut on their films. It was hardly a suitable finale for Audrey's big-screen career—if, indeed, it was the finale some expected it to be.

Another *Sabrina* star's career was gasping for breath. Bill Holden had made a string of unsuccessful films in the late 1970s, followed by a big-budget 1980 disaster, *When Time Ran Out,* in which he starred with Paul Newman. It was a failed attempt to re-create the success of *The Towering Inferno.* (Holden was only seven years older than Newman, who was still in high demand as a leading man.)

Now, in 1981, only a month before *They All Laughed* hit theaters, Bill Holden was starring on-screen with Audrey's onetime nemesis, Julie Andrews, in a controversial satire of the film industry, *S.O.B.,* in which Bill portrayed a director. The title didn't mean "son of a bitch" but rather "standard operational bullshit," referring to the usual misinformation emanating from Tinseltown. It was directed by *Breakfast at Tiffany's* Blake Edwards, who was married to Julie Andrews. Many years later, Andrews said that she did not think there was anyone who did not love Audrey, and that Blake Edwards "adored her, too. I think I can honestly say that if I hadn't come into his life, she might have." As for Bill, Julie said he was still a very sexy man.

S.O.B.'s concept was slightly reminiscent of *Paris When It Sizzles,* but much broader, edgier, and totally no-holds-barred. A key plot point called for forty-six-year-old Ms. Andrews to expose her breasts on-screen. As many pointed out, the stage's original Eliza Doolittle, Disney's Mary Poppins herself, and the star of the iconic *The Sound of Music*, had gone to great lengths indeed in trying to erase, once and for all, her "good girl" image. Tremendous publicity was generated, and Bill, Julie, and Blake went all-out promoting *S.O.B.*, but the movie failed to catch on.

Shortly after returning to Switzerland from New York, Audrey's mother suffered a stroke, her third. The baroness's health was deteriorating rapidly. But she liked and approved of Robert Wolders, and during her convalescence, they would often converse in Dutch. She was able to confide in him her deep feelings for her daughter, which she'd never been able to relay herself. Rob, in turn, would relate them to a grateful Audrey. The baroness could relax at last; Audrey had finally chosen the right man.

Audrey's relationship with "Robbie" was exactly what she wanted, and needed, and in a way had longed for since her divorce from Mel. That, for her, had been the ultimate low point, and she'd been miserable. But now, with Rob, she finally had a lover and a protector who truly cared about her, her welfare, and her happiness. He was tolerant, understanding, and kind. Most important, she could trust him. He would later point out the very real, and decidedly unglamorous, elements of their lives that bound them together in a way none of the other men in her life could possibly have fathomed. Both had lived through the Nazi occupation of Holland. They had suffered similar physical damage as a result. Through their formative years, there was often no access to doctors, dentists, or medicines; nutritious food was at best scarce, if available at all. At one point Audrey had baked green bread, consisting mainly of grass.

Children who survived, like Audrey and Rob, emerged with lifelong problems regarding their health, from head to toe. Reportedly, Rob sometimes suffered severe headaches and dizzy spells. Audrey had had to contend with one ailment or another her entire life. Her relationship with Rob was a mature one, rooted in reality. She was not only ready for it, she welcomed it. Their life together followed a very peaceful, orderly pattern. Walking their four Jack Russell terriers was one of the highlights of their day. Marriage was not a priority. "No, it's not important," Audrey later said. She considered herself "sort of married to Robert," and she saw no reason for marriage. The lack of it actually made their relationship seem more romantic.

Her happiness with Rob was evident to the camera. She looked beautiful at the American Film Institute tribute to her former co-star, Fred Astaire, praising him to the skies, omitting the truth—that it hadn't been pleasant working with him. At a black-tie event at the Reagan White House, wearing a gorgeous off-the-shoulder sheath gown and spectacular Bulgari earrings, she looked radiant with a handsome Rob by her side.

It was only a few months after the release of *They All Laughed* and *S.O.B.* that Audrey's original Hollywood Romeo made a sad, final appearance on the world stage.

~•~

Bill Holden was dead.

The news was everywhere, and the details were horrifying. This was not the way William Holden should have died. The public has fixed ideas on how their idols should go. If Princess Diana had stepped on a land mine, it would at least have been an understandable, dignified, ennobling way to die. Her real end was decidedly less so. Holden's death somehow evoked the image of him in *Sunset Boulevard*—his character,

Joe Gillis, dead, floating face down in the swimming pool and being fished out with hooks by the police.

The accepted version of events is that on November 12, 1981, Bill was drunk and alone in his high-rise apartment in Shore Cliff Towers on the seaside cliffs of Santa Monica, California. He was in his bedroom, slipped on a rug, and gashed his forehead on a bedside table. He began bleeding profusely and was conscious for at least thirty minutes after he fell. Whether he realized how seriously he was injured, and what he was thinking under the fog of alcohol, and when the numbness of unreality set in, will never be known. He did not summon aid—either because he was unable to, or as his friend Cliff Robertson later said, "He didn't want any help." The manager of the building, Bill Martin, noticed that he hadn't seen Holden in several days. Concerned, he let himself into the actor's apartment and discovered Holden's body. The coroner determined that he may have been dead for four days. The news broke on November 16.

Bill was dead? Audrey was stunned on hearing the news. She was in Paris, and the memories had to have come flooding back . . . what he'd been in the days when they were young and fresh and that magical chemistry passed between them. There were no public statements from Audrey. There was no way she'd intrude on Bill's family's privacy. She kept her sorrow to herself. Those close to her, who knew what she was feeling, kept her confidence.

On learning of Bill's demise, it was reported that Stefanie Powers collapsed. Production on her hit TV series *Hart to Hart* had to be temporarily shut down. Holden specified in his will that he did not want either a funeral—he considered them ghoulish—or a memorial service; he was to be cremated, his ashes scattered in the Pacific Ocean.

Powers organized a private gathering of friends to say their own good-byes to Bill. Holden contemporaries James Stewart and Richard

Widmark were present, along with Robert Wagner, Stefanie's co-star in *Hart to Hart*; Wagner's wife, Natalie Wood; Billy and Audrey Wilder; Lee Remick; Blake Edwards; Julie Andrews; Bill's goddaughter, Patti Davis, daughter of Nancy and Ronald Reagan—and Capucine.

Billy Wilder told *New York Times* reporter Stephen Farber that he'd really loved Bill, but it turned out he just didn't know him. "If somebody had said to me, 'Holden's dead,' I would have assumed that he had been gored by a water buffalo in Kenya, that he had died in a plane crash approaching Hong Kong, that a crazed jealous woman had shot him and he drowned in a swimming pool. But to be killed by a bottle of vodka and a night table—what a lousy fadeout for a great guy."

Wilder's epitaph for Holden brought into razor-sharp focus what Bill had always been about: "Here lies a very successful man, who spontaneously gave up his profession to devote himself to endangered species. He did not take much care of himself so he killed himself. However, what he neglected to consider was that he himself was an endangered species as well: The Handsome American."

Holden neighbor Bob Hope's comments, however, more or less reflected those of the general public: "I don't know what it was that caused these depressive moments when he would drink. His career was a success, he had friends and money. Who knows what causes those things?"

In Bill's will, Stefanie Powers received a $250,000 bequest, Capucine and Pat Stauffer $50,000 each; Ardis and their two sons, and Holden's niece, were all generously remembered as well.

Stefanie proved to be a worthy recipient of Bill's trust. Powers, along with Bill's business partners Don Hunt, Iris Breidenbend, and Dean Johnson, president of Warner Communications, established the William Holden Wildlife Foundation, which is still going strong today.

Bill was remembered in heartwarming fashion, by his dearest friend. On February 29, 1982, the Oscars were being held at the Dorothy Chandler Pavilion in Los Angeles. Johnny Carson was the host. Barbara Stanwyck was to be presented with an Honorary Academy Award, "for superlative creativity and unique contribution to the art of screen acting."

When a young John Travolta introduced her, she strode across the stage, ramrod straight, wearing a fitted, high-necked, long-sleeved red gown, her steel-gray hair beautifully coiffed. She received the only standing ovation of the evening. Travolta handed her the Oscar. When the audience quieted down, she thanked them, and began: "I tried many times to get it, but did not make it," the four-time nominee said. After thanking people she'd worked with over the years, she braced herself and concluded dramatically: "A few years ago, I stood on this stage with William Holden, as a presenter. I loved him very much and I miss him. He always wished that I would get an Oscar." She held up the statuette, her eyes filling with tears. "And so tonight, my Golden Boy, you've got your wish. . . ."

 ⌒•⌒

Audrey's father had died earlier in 1981, at age ninety-five. Although they had been in touch for years and she wrote him frequently and helped him financially, they were not close. She tried for some sort of emotional reconciliation, but they remained strangers, still awkward with each other. He was a cold man, and Audrey felt he never loved her. She knew William Wyler had loved her, and she felt the loss deeply when he, too, died that year.

In late September 1982, Audrey received a startling reminder of her own mortality. She and Grace Kelly were the same age, fifty-two. Grace had been driving with her daughter Stéphanie to Monaco from their country home, Roc Agel, on the French side of the border. Grace suffered a stroke, which caused her to drive her automobile off the road and down a mountainside. She was pulled alive from the wreckage but had suffered serious injuries and was unconscious. She died the following day, never having regained consciousness. Her daughter survived.

◀ *Courtesy Everett Collection*

▼ Audrey's great friend Capucine (in scarf), a star herself, visits the *Paris* set. She was now Bill's lover and often his caretaker (Bill, at right, is in the cowboy hat).

© *Bob Willoughby/ mptvimages.com*

▲ Audrey starred
with Cary Grant in
Charade (1963), a
romantic thriller in
which the two stars
never kissed (Grant,
twenty-four years
Audrey's senior, was
wary of seeming like
a lecherous older
man). Here, director
Stanley Donen
confers with his stars.

Courtesy Photofest

◄ A new kind of ordeal:
My Fair Lady (1964).
Director George
Cukor became one
of Audrey's closest
friends.

Courtesy Photofest

▲ Their on-screen chemistry was hardly in the Holden-Hepburn league, and Capucine was not *presented* properly. She and Bill made two films together, *The Lion* (1962) and *The Seventh Dawn* (1964).

Courtesy Photofest

◄ Audrey and Albert Finney starred in *Two for the Road* (1967). Off-camera, it was Holden redux.

Courtesy Photofest

▲ Dream girls Grace and Audrey, almost a decade after their affairs with Bill. L. to R.: Grace, Prince Rainier, Audrey, and Mel, at a 1965 charity benefit for elderly actors. Both women were thirty-six, Audrey still at a career peak. Grace longed to return to the screen.

Courtesy Photofest

◄ Mel Ferrer visits his wife on the set of *Wait Until Dark* (1967). A divorce was finally on the horizon.

Courtesy Photofest

▲ Audrey, a few months
shy of forty, marries
her second husband,
Dr. Andrea Dotti, on
January 1, 1969. He was
nine years younger.
She now had two titles:
baroness, which she was
born with, and countess.

Courtesy Photofest

▶ Capucine visits Audrey,
wheeling a baby
carriage, in Gstaad,
Switzerland. Hepburn
had achieved her
longed-for wish: she had
given birth to a second
child, Luca. Older
son, Sean, now had a
half brother.

*Rex Features/Courtesy
Everett Collection*

◀ Holden with mentor Barbara Stanwyck, over forty years after she'd helped him through their 1939 film, *Golden Boy*. Although she was fourteen years his senior, she'd outlive him by almost a decade.

Courtesy Photofest

▼ With Ben Gazzara during production of *They All Laughed* (1981). Her hopes of reigniting the passion they'd shared during production of *Bloodline*, a couple of years earlier, were in vain.

Courtesy Photofest

◄ With Robert
Wolders, the last
great love of her life.

© Image Collect.com/
Acepixs

▼ Holden with Stefanie
Powers, the last
great love of his life.
He was twenty-four
years older.

© ImageCollect.com/
Globe-Photos

▲ All the passion and perseverance that had gone into her career, and raising her children, now went into Audrey's efforts to promote UNICEF.

UNICEF/ Hulton Archive/Getty Images

◀ Similar to Audrey with UNICEF, wildlife preservation became Bill's great charitable endeavor.

Courtesy Photofest

PART IV

Here's to Life

Chapter

17

"M IND IF I SMOKE?"
"Yes!" Audrey, lifetime smoker, answered emphatically, and totally credibly. It was an exchange of dialogue between her and Robert Wagner in the big-budget movie-for-television they were making in 1986, *Love Among Thieves*.

She'd decided to go back to work; the last few years had been tough indeed. There had been good news in the summer of 1982, when her divorce decree became final. But after that, a series of unhappy events: dear friend George Cukor had died in 1983; the death of her mother, the following year, was devastating. Audrey felt lost without her. Although their relationship had not been smooth, it was always supportive and, in its own way, loving.

Work was a godsend. She didn't mind that it was television. Mel had struck financial gold as one of the stars of the hit series *Falcon Crest*, which was going strong at the time. And Audrey was not exactly a stranger to the medium. *Mayerling*, with Mel, had been produced at the very peak of her stardom, and that had been done "live." Other top stars and directors were doing movies for the small screen, including Katharine Hepburn, Laurence Olivier, Paul Newman, and Joanne Woodward (Newman as director). *Love Among Thieves*, a romantic adventure comedy, was a project tailored for Audrey.

Robert ("R. J.") Wagner would be her leading man. He was riding the crest of his TV fame, thanks to *Hart to Hart,* the series co-starring Stefanie Powers. Back in 1981, barely two weeks after Holden's death, Wagner had suffered his own experience from hell: his wife, Natalie Wood, drowned in the waters off Catalina Island. The circumstances were as chilling as they'd been with Bill.

Five years had passed. *Love Among Thieves* was designed to be a romp for Wagner and Audrey. He was thrilled to be starring with her; she had no greater fan. He'd known her for years, and liked and respected everything about her—her lifestyle, her personal style, but most of all her loyalty to her friends.

Their mutual friend Capucine, with whom Wagner had co-starred decades earlier in *The Pink Panther,* was at a low ebb. Bill's death, and Charlie Feldman's, had hit her hard. Her protectors were gone. Audrey was always there for her, and always tried to help. Her gentle pep talks brought some stability into her life. And, fortunately, Cap was active professionally. There had been featured roles in *Pink Panther* sequels, appearances on *Hart to Hart; Murder, She Wrote;* and other TV work. But she was terrified of growing old.

Love Among Thieves was filmed on locations all over the West Coast. Audrey certainly brought out the best in Wagner as an actor; he'd never been so open and direct. He grew a scruffy beard for his role. His fans, and, no doubt, his network bosses, were accustomed to a clean-shaven, sartorially perfect Wagner.

Audrey was nervous about doing the film. She had been offscreen for over five years, and getting back into the routine at the age of fifty-seven was a daunting process. Film acting, for her, was not emotions, but thinking, and required intense concentration. There was a lot of dialogue to memorize, and the pace of shooting a movie for TV was fast. Legendary ballet dancer Mikhail Baryshnikov, who'd made the transition to film actor at the age of twenty-nine, said he found acting exhausting because of the need to hold the emotional level all day long. He said it was easier to do a full-length ballet than to sustain emotionality during the waiting hours of a shooting day.

Audrey's insecurity made itself known when she confided to director Roger Young that she was relying on his help, because Wagner was such an experienced television performer. She looked good. Her walk, at times, seemed to have taken on a slightly irregular stride, which many former ballerinas, at Audrey's age, had to contend with. Comparisons with Audrey's younger self were always inevitable. Before long, however, studio executives were insisting that she play this role à la Holly Golightly. *Breakfast at Tiffany's* had been made twenty-five years earlier. This was not a welcome development.

Audrey was faced with a variation of the situation Cary Grant had had to contend with when they had made *Charade*. In that instance, he didn't want to look foolish opposite a much younger leading lady. Coincidentally, Audrey was now close to the age Grant was when they'd done the film. Audrey and Wagner were virtually the same age, so that wasn't the problem; it simply seemed as through the front office wanted a twenty-five-year-old Audrey to play opposite him. The demand placed additional pressure on her and didn't enhance what should have been a memorable working experience. She rose to the occasion, as always, and hit all the right notes as a glamorous, sophisticated thief, a classical pianist and baroness. This would be the first time Audrey played a titled character. Some of her clothes, usually timelessly contemporary, reflected the times: the exaggerated broad-shoulders-look characterized several of her dresses. Only her evening gowns were by Givenchy.

The final scene in *Love Among Thieves* was memorable, an homage to Audrey's famous fashion-shoot sequence in *Funny Face*, where, with the awe-inspiring "Winged Victory" sculpture as her backdrop, she descended the stairs of the Louvre, breathtakingly gowned, arms outstretched, telling photographer Astaire, "Take the picture! Take the picture!" In this case, it wasn't the Louvre but a suitable American look-alike (minus "Winged Victory"). Givenchy had created for her a stunning red sheath gown, a work of art, pure Audrey. Red might have been her least favorite color, but she couldn't have looked more fantastic as she walked down those stairs.

Audrey obviously could successfully be made to look as she did in her youth—or close to it—if all elements were in place to present her properly. It was too bad a deal had fallen through for Ross Hunter to produce a picture with her. He was a master at showcasing female stars who had reached a certain age. There would have been many scenes like the final one in *Love Among Thieves*, and Hepburn fans, and possibly Audrey herself, would have been ecstatic. "I adore Audrey," Hunter had said, on many occasions, over the years. But obviously, both producer and star had waited too long to get a project underway.

Love Among Thieves was not the end of the professional road; Audrey would soon make her final big-screen appearance. But a new passion had taken the prominent position in her life. It assumed an importance that, as far as she was concerned, totally eclipsed any show-business venture.

∽•∽

Her new calling was a humanitarian endeavor. Audrey once said, "For me, the only things of interest are those linked to the heart." Her sons were now adults, so she was free to travel. With Rob by her side: "He's so good to me, he takes great care of me, and it's a wonderful feeling to love somebody, to be loved." She would travel extensively as an

International Goodwill Ambassador for UNICEF (United Nations International Children's Emergency Fund). Movies would have to step aside for yet another passion in her ever-changing universe.

She was thrilled that she had found a constructive use for her fame. People paid attention to what Audrey Hepburn had to say, and her message was clear: "It's that wonderful, old-fashioned idea that others come first and you come second. This was the ethic by which I was brought up. Others matter more than you do, so 'Don't fuss, dear, get on with it,'" as her late mother used to tell her.

She'd assumed the UNICEF post in 1988, at a salary of $1 per year. At the age of fifty-nine, she applied the same focus, discipline, and determination to this task as she had when, as a young girl, she'd trained vigorously to become a ballerina, then an actress. Ballet had been a world of physical pain. She'd experienced that; and she'd seen firsthand the physical and psychological pain suffered by the poor and displaced children of the world. "I've known what it is to be hungry and afraid," she said.

"Personally, I can do very little, but I can contribute to a whole chain of events, and that's a marvelous feeling. It's like a bonus to me towards the end of my life. It gives me a voice." She addressed special assemblies of the United Nations and world parliaments, and was totally involved in preparing the speeches, which were written out in large print so she could avoid wearing her glasses. She was ill at ease speaking in public. "Acting is quite different from getting up in front of people," she explained, and to calm her nerves, she would have a cup of coffee; sometimes, a shot of bourbon.

Manfred Faridi, who worked at the UN, recalled attending one of her speeches, and he was impressed. "She had a very expressive manner, you knew she was speaking sincerely, from the heart. Many speakers were stiff, and unconvincing, they were just reading words. With

Ms. Hepburn, it was exactly the opposite. I suppose it was a big help that she was a professional actress."

In fact, it wasn't—she had no character to inhabit or interpret; she was totally on her own, presenting herself. It was an ordeal. Her aim was simple and straightforward: to make a difference, and Rob made it clear that Audrey "was not trying to be Mother Teresa, or vying for saint-hood." Rob coordinated Audrey's activities and ran interference, and Audrey said she couldn't have done it without him. He was functioning just as Mel had—without any of Mel's drawbacks.

Her travels took her to dozens of UNICEF-assisted projects in Sudan, El Salvador, Honduras, Mexico, Venezuela, Ecuador, Bangladesh, Vietnam, Thailand, Ethiopia, Sudan, Eritrea, and Somalia. She wore no makeup, but she always flashed that Hepburn smile, and photographs of her with the children appeared all over the world.

Travel was difficult, no-frills at best, usually highly uncomfortable, and conditions at their destinations were often "a living nightmare." This was no case of a movie star disembarking from a limo, making a fast appearance, and dashing off to the next photo opportunity. In addi-tion, Audrey and Rob had had to have a series of painful immunization injections; infectious diseases were rampant in many territories. It was risky, especially for a couple who had their own health concerns.

She not only posed for pictures; on occasion, she was permitted to vaccinate babies. The children, to quote one account, "followed her like the Pied Piper," and in their faces, she saw something of her-self. Her own face often betrayed her fatigue, one journalist noting that she was "clearly ragged with exhaustion." But she was having an impact and felt revitalized. She experienced a new sense of purpose. She said that she had little interest in making any more films. The fun had gone out of it.

Stanley Donen, recalling how focused she'd once been on her career, "and its gratifications," observed quite a change in Audrey—she'd grown up, "she's come of age and entered another stage of life."

She agreed to be a presenter at the Oscars with Gregory Peck—a great reunion, and an equally great opportunity, during interviews, to talk about UNICEF. Peck was now seventy-two; his formerly very young co-star was now fifty-nine, and they still looked wonderful together. Presenting the writing awards, amid the current crop of stars, she moved critic Janet Maslin to write that she and Peck stood out like "visiting royalty."

Around this time, Audrey received an offer to return to the screen; it turned out to be one she couldn't possibly turn down. The offer came from director Steven Spielberg. The forty-three-year-old Wonder Boy had been the auteur of a series of staggeringly successful films, including *Jaws, Close Encounters of the Third Kind, Raiders of the Lost Ark, E.T., The Color Purple,* and *Back to the Future.* Spielberg wanted Audrey for an important cameo role in his new film, *Always.* It was a World War II romantic drama, a remake of the classic 1943 film *A Guy Named Joe,* one of Spielberg's favorite movies, which had starred Spencer Tracy, Irene Dunne, and Van Johnson. The director had been the great Victor Fleming, whose triumphs included *Gone with the Wind.*

Richard Dreyfuss, Holly Hunter, and John Goodman were among the stars of the Spielberg version, although Spielberg himself was the biggest drawing card. Audrey would be portraying an otherworldly being, an angel, "Hap." During the course of the story, she explains to Pete (Dreyfuss), a slain pilot, that he must provide Spiritus ("the divine breath") to others. "They hear you inside their own minds as if it were their thoughts," she tells him. "You've had your life, and anything you do for yourself is a waste of spirit."

Her scenes would be shot in less than two weeks, for which she would be paid a reported $1 million. The film, unlike Spielberg's previous big-budgeters, was produced on a smaller scale but was still a fantasy—one that subsequently inspired a slew of similar genre films, including *Ghost*. The Hepburn persona would provide an added touch of gentle dignity, and a jolt of superstar power, especially in foreign markets. She'd be dressed in white, with a cowl-necked, long-sleeved top worn over tailored slacks. Her hair was smoothed back from her face, just as she always wore it in those days. She would be carefully photographed. She seemed fragile and tired. But her voice was vintage Hepburn, no trace of coarseness even after decades of smoking. And on-screen, her characterization as always came to proper life.

Dreyfuss, Hunter, and Goodman were big names at the time and were prominently featured in the posters. Audrey, on this occasion, was the extra added attraction.

~•~

As she approached her sixtieth birthday, an inner serenity seemed to counterbalance her hectic life. She was still asked the usual, non-UNICEF-related questions: did she know how wonderful-looking she was? From teenagers of her own generation, to opera singer Maria Callas, to Barbara Walters, to teenagers of today, the Hepburn "look" remained—and remains—sought after. She patiently replied that she never looked in the mirror and thought to herself, "How wonderful I look!" What she did see were many imperfections, features she was still not thrilled with (she wished she had a smaller nose), and in order to compensate and correct, "I did make an effort!" She was aware that people didn't want her to age. They wanted her to be the eternal ingenue. But how, she asked, could one survive the chaos of life, its mountains of difficulties, and remain an ingenue? One thing Audrey was adamant about: she didn't believe in exercise—that was too much like school: "I like to be free. There are too many musts in life without adding exercise."

By this point, she was uncomfortable talking about her personal life. "My mother wouldn't approve!" she exclaimed. And there was that other perennial query: why was she so thin? Her current weight, at age sixty, was 110 pounds. She was born thin, she said, and pointed out that she always ate hearty meals and denied herself no particular food; in fact, she loved chocolate.

No, she had no regrets about the films she had turned down that went on to become big hits. "That wouldn't make any sense," she said. "That's the way my life went. I don't regret giving up the movies for my children. If it went the other way around, I'd be miserable today. If I had only movies to look back on, I'd never have known my boys." There was never a question: "I couldn't take the stress of being away from my sons," she explained. "I missed them too much. I became emotionally unhappy. Some people can deal with that. It is not easy." She had great admiration for those women who could seemingly have a big career while at the same time taking care of their husbands and children. As far as Audrey was concerned: "I cannot deal with too many emotions."

She had no thoughts of retirement. "I don't think I'll retire 'til I die." She didn't care that people knew her age. What was important to her was that she not feel old. "When you can't contribute anymore, that's when you start feeling old and that is the beginning of the end."

Sadly, that end wasn't far off. Everything had been going along beautifully. Gregory Peck presented her with the Cecil B. DeMille Award at the 1990 Golden Globes ceremonies. "Elegant, radiant, incandescent—there aren't enough adjectives to describe her," Peck said, in his most sonorous tones, in his introduction.

That evening she looked sensational in a cream satin, high-necked, long-sleeved sheath, and her makeup, for a change, was not pastel-hued. Despite her aversion to the color red, her lipstick was crimson and it was extremely flattering. She looked younger and more vibrant at this public event than she had in years. The speech she gave was interesting—all her recent experience as a public speaker had paid off. She touched on her beginnings ("Years ago, I got a great start . . . "), and without mentioning UNICEF, she thanked the media for calling attention to the plight of others, then said there wasn't enough time to thank all those who had made her career possible.

She proceeded to rattle off the names of all her directors, including the most recent, and her leading men, Bill included, of course (she called him William on this occasion), concluding with "Fred Astaire," who had died two years earlier. Her diction was crystal clear and every name came through. The speeded-up delivery was clearly intentional, and she smiled when she received the response she had hoped for—laughter and applause. It was a light note in what was otherwise a serious speech. She also thanked her agent of thirty-five years, Kurt Frings.

During her remarks, the camera cut away to Rob in the audience, bearded, very handsome, and intense in black tie, sipping champagne. The on-screen graphic incorrectly identified him as: Robert Wolders (Audrey Hepburn's Husband).

Looking the way she did that night, producers and directors must have scurried to contact Frings to see which of their projects she might fit into. Audrey wasn't tempted.

That year, another tragedy: Capucine had reached her breaking point. How many times had she wept and said her life was over? But the pain had finally become too much, and she jumped to her death from the window of her eighth-floor apartment in Lausanne, where she and Bill had once spent so much time together. To Audrey, and those who loved Cap, it was a heartrending blow.

$\sim \cdot \subset$

Audrey's humanitarian interests assumed more importance than ever. In addition to her UNICEF commitments, she agreed to headline a special project: *Gardens of the World*, an eight-part documentary series for PBS. Like the late Princess Grace, Audrey adored flowers and gardening (a tulip was named in her honor). The series would require three months of travel.

Behind the scenes, an unexpected scenario took place: Audrey did her own hair ("All I need is a hair dryer," she said), makeup, and wardrobe. It would save production costs, although the producers had already factored in the cost of a personal hairdresser, makeup artist, wardrobe person, and secretary. And Audrey donated her entire fee, plus thousands of dollars of her own, to UNICEF.

In the spring of 1991, she was honored by the Film Society of Lincoln Center. In her speech, her voice betraying a hint of nervousness, she got the laugh she was hoping for when she said: "I think it's quite wonderful that this skinny broad could be turned into a marketable commodity. . . ."

A year later, fund-raising for UNICEF in Europe, she didn't feel quite right, and she didn't look well. It was assumed that she had picked up some virulent bug during her extensive travels. Her doctors prescribed medication; she experienced bad side effects and afterward didn't feel any better. Further tests were performed, producing no specific diagnosis. But more tests, unfortunately, did: in November, she learned she had cancer, and it was widespread. Rob was literally stunned. It was Audrey's son Sean who told her the news. She seemed to have anticipated it, and there were no hysterics.

She underwent chemotherapy treatments, then rallied, but soon her condition worsened. She underwent two surgeries. She was disappointed that a third would not be possible. Rob later revealed that neither he nor her sons could acknowledge that she was dying.

Only a few years earlier, Audrey had been asked if she was happy. She said she was very happy. "Took a while," she laughed, "but I got there." She recognized the incredible good fortune she'd enjoyed: "My own life has been much more than a fairy tale," she said. "I've had my share of difficult moments, but whatever difficulties I've gone through, I've always gotten a prize at the end." She was the first to note: "I probably hold the distinction of being one movie star who, by all laws of logic, should never have made it. At each stage of my career, I lacked the experience."

Director Billy Wilder had outlived Bill Holden and virtually all the other stars he'd worked with. And he would outlive Audrey. He'd been particularly fond of Hepburn and Holden. Late in life, he said: "They both had great careers, but unhappy private lives." Holden's, indisputably; but, in love with Audrey, he had hoped that maybe she could have rescued him from his more harmful inclinations.

Audrey's private life—that was another story. She'd never ended her search for what she described as that light at the end of the tunnel. Based on her correspondence and the many conversations she had with friends, relatives, and, of course, the press over recent years, she'd truly felt she'd found it.

She died on January 20, 1993, at her beloved home in Tolochenaz. It was not a soft-focus exit; quite the opposite. She was surrounded by family. Sons Sean and Luca; her devoted "Robbie"; and Mel and Andrea were on hand. Givenchy came to see her; he'd arranged for the private plane that had flown Audrey and her family to Switzerland, where she wanted to spend her last days. It was an indescribably sorrowful and painful ordeal for all concerned. Sean later noted, "She wasn't angry . . . she felt at peace with it. She felt that death is a natural part of life."

For Hollywood historians, it is an interesting coincidence that Audrey and Bill each died at the same age: sixty-three. Their personas, in the prime of their lives when they were deeply in love—the days when all seemed possible—live on in *Sabrina*. For Audrey's new generations of fans, that film remains, even more than *Roman Holiday*, the signature film of her early career. Her iconic image was formed in *Sabrina*—the way she looked, dressed, and the chemistry between the stars. These were timeless.

Bill Holden's impact influenced succeeding generations of actors, and for some he was among the most admired actors of Hollywood's Golden Age. Alec Baldwin has noted: "There's three things: there's masculinity, there's intelligence, there's sensitivity. You've got to bring those three things to a leading man's role: masculinity, sensitivity, intelligence. In some people there's a little too much in the mix of one or the other. With Holden it was always the perfect mix."

From the beginning, Audrey and Bill were wildly successful in their profession. Later, both found deeply meaningful avocations that brought them great satisfaction, Hepburn with UNICEF, Holden with wildlife preservation.

Both possessed, in abundance, "that little something extra" that defines star quality. Although they both died relatively young, and their love story came to an end, thanks to *Sabrina*, we will always have the romance.

SELECT BIBLIOGRAPHY

Bacall, Lauren. *By Myself.* Knopf, 1978.

Barbour, Alan G. *Humphrey Bogart.* Galahad Books, 1973.

Beaton, Cecil. *Cecil Beaton: Portraits and Profiles.* Edited by Hugo Vickers. Frances Lincoln, 2014.

———. *Cecil Beaton's Fair Lady.* Henry Holt, 1964.

———. *The Unexpurgated Beaton: The Cecil Beaton Diaries, As He Wrote Them.* Deckle Edge, 2003.

Capua, Michelangelo. *William Holden: A Biography.* McFarland, 2010.

Cooper, Jackie, with Dick Kleiner. *Please Don't Shoot My Dog: An Autobiography.* William Morrow, 1981.

Crosby, Gary, with Ross Firestone. *Going My Own Way.* Doubleday, 1983.

Crowe, Cameron. *Conversations with Wilder.* Faber and Faber, 1999.

Dunaway, Faye. *Looking for Gatsby: My Life.* Simon and Schuster, 1995.

Ferrer, Sean Hepburn. *Audrey Hepburn: An Elegant Spirit.* Atria Books, 2003.

Gazzara, Ben. *In the Moment: My Life as an Actor.* Carroll and Graf, 2004.

Griggs, John. *The Films of Gregory Peck.* Introduction by Judith Crist. Citadel Press, 1984.

Hanna, David. *Ava: A Portrait of a Star.* G. P. Putnam's Sons, 1960.

Head, Edith, with Paddy Calistro. *Edith Head's Hollywood.* Dutton, 1983.

Higham, Charles. *Audrey: The Life of Audrey Hepburn.* Macmillan, 1984.

Lambert, Gavin. *On Cukor.* G. P. Putnam's Sons, 1972.

Logan, Joshua. *Josh: My Up and Down, In and Out Life.* Delacorte Press, 1976.

———. *Movie Stars, Real People and Me.* Delacorte Press, 1978.

Loos, Anita. *A Cast of Thousands.* Grosset and Dunlap, 1997.

Morley, Sheridan. *Audrey Hepburn: A Celebration.* Pavilion, 1993.

Myers, Jeffrey. *Bogart: A Life in Hollywood.* Houghton Mifflin, 1997.

Paris, Barry. *Audrey Hepburn.* Putnam, 1996.

Parish, James Robert, and Don E. Stanke. *The All-Americans.* Arlington House, 1977.

Payn, Graham, and Sheridan Morley, eds. *The Noel Coward Diaries.* Weidenfeld and Nicolson, 1982.

Powers, Stefanie. *One from the Hart.* Simon and Schuster, 2011.

Quine, Judith Balaban. *The Bridesmaids: Grace Kelly, Princess of Monaco, and Six Intimate Friends.* Weidenfeld and Nicolson, 1989.

Reagan, Ronald. *Where's the Rest of Me?* Sloan and Pierce, 1965.

Silverman, Stephen M. *Dancing on the Ceiling: Stanley Donen and His Movies.* Knopf, 1996.

Spada, James. *Grace: The Secret Lives of a Princess.* Doubleday, 1987.

Spoto, Donald. *Enchantment: The Life of Audrey Hepburn.* Harmony Books, 2006.

Swanson, Gloria. *Swanson on Swanson.* Random House, 1980.

Thomas, Bob. *Golden Boy: The Untold Story of William Holden.* St. Martin's Press, 1983.

Thomson, Charles. *Bing: The Unauthorized Biography.* David McKay, 1975.

Thomson, Verita. *Bogie and Me.* St. Martin's Press, 1982.

Wagner, Robert. *Pieces of My Heart: A Life.* Harper Collins, 2008.

Walker, Alexander. *Audrey Hepburn: Her Real Story.* St. Martin's Press, 1994.

Wallis Hyer, Martha. *Finding My Way.* Harper San Francisco, 1990.

Wayne, Jane Ellen. *Grace Kelly's Men.* St. Martin's Press, 1991.

Wilkerson, Tichi, and Marcia Borie. *The Hollywood Reporter.* Coward-McCann, 1984.

Wilson, Victoria. *A Life of Barbara Stanwyck: Steel-True, 1907–1940.* Simon and Schuster, 2013.

Zolotow, Maurice. *Billy Wilder in Hollywood.* G. P. Putnam's Sons, 1977.

ACKNOWLEDGMENTS

HANK YOU TO THE MANY INDIVIDUALS OVER THE YEARS who provided insight and information regarding the fascinating lives and times of Audrey Hepburn and William Holden; people who knew what really went on behind the scenes and who weren't shy about answering the questions of a young publicist, a native New Yorker recently graduated from New York University who had an insatiable curiosity about stars, films, and Hollywood.

As New York press contact for MCA/Universal for well over a decade, and author (or co-author) of twenty books ranging from such subjects as Paul Newman and Joanne Woodward to Clara Bow, the original "It" Girl, I had the unique opportunity of meeting, working with, and spending "insider" time with many who were one-of-a-kind in their respective fields, both in front of and behind the cameras, including legendary reporters and PR executives, John Springer and his lovely wife, June, prominent among the latter. Their recollections never failed to spark my curiosity. Interesting how, during the 1960s and 1970s, when the movie business was changing so dramatically, questions regarding the "old days" to industry veterans who were still functioning in top capacities brought forth an enthusiasm—indeed, passion—that was somewhat lacking regarding the then "current" scene.

Jennings Lang, Billy Wilder, Alfred Hitchcock, George Seaton, Hal Wallis, Martin Rackin, Ross Hunter, and David Brown were spellbinding raconteurs. Jerry (Jerome B.) Evans, whose association with Universal before MCA's takeover in the 1960s went back to the late 1940s, Paul Kamey, Bernie (Bernard) Serlin, Fortunat Baronat, Bob Ungerfeld, Milton Livingston, Herman Kass, Bernie (Bernard) Korban, and Dick Delson were the well-connected PR executives in New York who, along with their West Coast counterparts, kept MCA/Universal front and center in the public's mind. And all of us were kept informed, via our counterparts at other studios, as to exactly what was happening in all corners of the industry. It was an invaluable education and has proven to be a great asset for my career as an author.

Presiding over MCA/Universal was the iconic Lew Wasserman. Visiting studio executives from the West Coast, and from overseas, always had colorful off-the-record anecdotes, complaints, and so on, to report; many of these men had been, and in some cases were still, instrumental in the careers (and lives) of a number of great stars, including not only Audrey and Bill, but Marlon Brando, Marilyn Monroe, Dean Martin, Jerry Lewis, Grace Kelly, and a host of others.

Earl Wilson, one of the best of the veteran show business columnist-reporters, was not only a close personal contact but a veritable gold mine of anecdotes, as was Gannett Newspapers entertainment guru (and former protégé of Dashiel Hammett) Bernie (Bernard) Drew. Thank you to Pat Gaston Manville, a wonderful friend whose experiences, insight, and intelligence matched her striking beauty. And thank you to Teet Carle, Anita Colby Flagler, Adela Rogers St. Johns, Hal Boyle, Alice Hughes, Doug Anderson, and Johnny Madden.

And to the individuals I spoke to, and in some cases worked with, long before *Audrey and Bill* became a reality, including Joshua Logan, Dore Schary, Eddie Albert, Charlton Heston, Shelley Winters, Cliff

Robertson, Gregory Peck, Bert Stern, and Gloria Swanson and her husband, writer William Dufty.

Renowned critic Judith Crist and husband Bill's annual "Survival" parties, in their Riverside Drive apartment in New York, brought together a potpourri of show-business insiders, past and present, whose intimate knowledge of the goings-on in the world of films and theater always left one much wiser, to say the least, by the end of the evening (more accurately, the early hours of the next morning).

Thank you to Edith Head and Sheilah Graham for that memorable, intimate winter afternoon tea in an almost deserted Edwardian Room of the Plaza Hotel. With their mile-a-minute chatter, and cutting-edge observations, the two women would have struck gold in today's reality TV marketplace.

For their support and help, special thanks to Joan Perry, Chris Kachulis, Lou Valentino, Scott Schwartz, Jeffrey Ziffer, and Phyllis Schwartz.

My sincere gratitude to my great editor, Cindy De La Hoz; and to production editor Cisca Schreefel.

Many thanks to my agent, Eric Myers.

INDEX